JUSTICE FOR 1971
WAR RAPES

Trial and Beyond

TUREEN AFROZ

PARTRIDGE

ISBN: Softcover   978-1-5437-5891-7
            eBook   978-1-5437-5892-4

Print information available on the last page.

To order additional copies of this book, contact
Toll Free +65 3165 7531 (Singapore)
Toll Free +60 3 3099 4412 (Malaysia)
orders.singapore@partridgepublishing.com

www.partridgepublishing.com/singapore

CONTENTS

List of Tables

Dedication

This research is dedicated to the

war rape victims of the world.

Acknowledgement

This work would not have been possible without the financial support of the East West University Centre for Research and Training (EWUCRT).

I am grateful to all of those with whom I have had the pleasure to work with. Specifically, I would like to express my special thanks of gratitude to **Md. Pizuar Hossain**, Senior Lecturer, Department of Law, East West University, Bangladesh for his tremendous assistance in discussing the relevant issues, and providing critical comments that greatly improved the quality of this research work. I am also grateful to **Mr. Farabi Bin Zahir**, Freelance Researcher and Columnist for his gigantic effort in locating the war rape victims all over Bangladesh. It has been the toughest part of this research work to actually locate the war rape victims and to arrange to conduct the survey in all 8 divisions of Bangladesh. I have been immensely benefitted by the last moment proof-reading by the researcher **Ms. Esrat Jahan Siddiki**.

I express my utmost gratitude to the **UGC Professor Dr. Fakrul Alam**, Department of English, University of Dhaka for kindly agreeing to take some time out from his immensely busy schedule to do the final editing.

I express my sincere gratitude to various national and international scholars, academics, activists, and practitioners who offered their valuable comments and critics during many national and international conferences in which I presented various parts of my research work included in this book. Some of them also provided me one-to-one guidance to fine-tune many of the arguments presented in this book. I would like to explicitly mention some of their names, such as (in alphabetical order) *Dr. Adam Jones*, Professor of Political Science, University of British Columbia (Canada); *Judge Agnieszka Klonowiecka-Milart* of the Extraordinary Chambers in the Courts of Cambodia (Cambodia); *Dr. Alexander Hinton*, Director of the Centre for the Study of Genocide and Human Rights, Professor of Anthropology, and UNESCO Chair in Genocide Prevention at Rutgers University, Newark (USA); *Dr. Anuradha Rai*, Assistant Professor of the Amity University (India); *Dr. Daniel Feierstein*, President of the International Association of Genocide Scholars, Director of the Centre of Genocide Studies at the National University of Tres de Febrero in Buenos Aires, Argentina, Professor of the University of Buenos Aires and National University of Tres de Febrero (Argentina); *Judge Daniel Horacio Obligado*, a Member of the Argentinean Tribunal (Argentina); *Ms. Elizabeth Silkes*, Director, International Coalition of Sites of Conscience (USA); *Late Ms. Ferdousi Priyobhashini*, Sculptist (Bangladesh); *Dr. Helen Jarvis*, Advisor to the Royal Government of Cambodia (Cambodia); *Mr. Helmut Scholz*, a Member of the European Union Parliament (Germany); *Mr. Hiranmoy Karlekar*, Consultant Editor of *The Pioneer* and former Editor of *Hindustan Times* (India); *Dr. Irene Victoria Massimino*, Professor, University of Lomas de Zamora (Argentina); *Dr. Jayanta Kumar Ray*, National Research Professor, Government of India (India); *Dr. Katharina Hoffmann*, Member of the Working Group Migration – Gender – Politics at Carl Von Ossietzky University Oldenburg (Germany); *Mrs. Maleka Khan*, Social Activist (Bangladesh); *Mr. Man Sokkoeun*, Human Rights Activist (Cambodia); *Mr. Manosh Ghosh*, Journalist (India); *Mr.*

Michel Gottret, Special Adviser to the Task Force for Dealing with the Past (Switzerland); *Ms. Mina Watanabe*, Secretary General of the Women's Active Museum on War and Peace (Tokyo); *Mr. Mohssen Arishie*, Managing Editor, Egyptian Gazette (Egypt); *Mr. Niran Anketell*, Attorney at Law and Director, South Asian Centre for Legal Studies, Colombo (Sri Lanka); *Mr. Paulo Casaca*, Founder and Executive Director, South Asia Democratic Forum and a former member of the European Parliament (Belgium); *Dr. Mohammad Salim*, Professor of History, Jagannath University (Bangladesh); *Mr. Sheikh Hafizur Rahman*, Associate Professor, Department of Law, University of Dhaka (Bangladesh); *Mr. Thomas A. Dine*, Faculty Member, Prague Leadership Institute (Czech Republic); *Dr. Trudy Huskamp Peterson*, Archival Consultant and Certified Archivist (USA); and *Ms. Umme Wara Mishu*, Assistant Professor, Department of Criminology, University of Dhaka (Bangladesh).

Above all, I want to thank my only child, *Tejoshwee Tureen (Shumedha)*, who means the world to me.

Tureen Afroz

Abstract

The history of 1971 Bangladesh War of Liberation accords the mass rape of Bangladeshi women by the Pakistan Army and their local collaborators. There is evidence that along with rape of the Bangladeshi women, other forms of sexual violence such as sexual slavery, enforced prostitution, and forced pregnancy were also committed by the perpetrators. After about 40 years of our Liberation War, the matter of rape of the Bangladeshi women was brought under litigation, to a certain extent, in the International Crimes Tribunal of Bangladesh (ICT-BD).

The *Constitution of the People's Republic of Bangladesh* is the supreme law of Bangladesh. It explicitly declares in its preamble that Bangladesh should establish a society where '... the rule of law, fundamental human rights and freedom, equality and justice, political, economic and social, will be secured for all citizens'. The aspect of "equality and justice" is lucidly presented along with the social issue. Thus, our constitution emphasizes the kind of justice which is "complete justice" and provides assurance of both legal justice and social justice. In this context, one notes that the issue of justice for the rape victims of the 1971 Bangladesh War of Liberation still lacks comprehensive social and legal attention.

By now a number of war criminals of the Liberation War of Bangladesh are being punished by the ICT-BD. Through this process, it may assume that even though justice had been delayed, it was ultimately not denied. However, a question remained unexplored as to whether *'legal justice'* essentially ensures *'social justice'* for the war rape victims in our country. It has been observed that the war rape victims are still not socially recognized and/or respected; rather, they are considered as outcasts in our society. Unfortunately, nobody knows as to how justice is being perceived by them. Thus, it remains an unspoken narrative in our country in respect of how the war rape victims actually perceive 'justice'. Another question that arises in this regard is whether *'complete justice'* is being done in the course of ensuring legal justice to war rape victims. Hence, it can be questioned as to how far 'justice' is being done to the war rape victims of Bangladesh by conducting trials of war criminals?

This research would endeavor to get an account from the war rape victims and their families about the socio-legal aspects of the long-awaited justice. It may be mentioned that no systematic and/or comprehensive research has been conducted so far on this subject. This research is of significance because even after a remarkable number of convictions of the perpetrators by the ICT-BD and the Appellate Division of the Supreme Court of Bangladesh, it is still not clear how much justice is being done to victims in Bangladesh from socio-legal perspectives. We should not forget, '[n]ot only must Justice be done; it must also be seen to be done.' Hence, this research has covered surveying total 385 rape victims (and their families) of total 53 Districts of all the 8 Divisions of Bangladesh.

To conclude, it can be stated that the sexual violence and rape, committed whether during war or peacetime, was widespread and that the women were often victimized by Pakistani men and their collaborators. The experience of 1971 Liberation War of Bangladesh, when perpetrators used the rape of women as a war tactic, is hardly discussed in the international arena. However, a growing number of cases recognizing war rape as an illegal act have been taken up partly as a result of the heinous use of rape as a tactic of genocide in both Rwanda and Yugoslavia during 1990s. This study has described various legal mechanisms to hold the perpetrators of sexual violence liable under the IHL, the ICHL, decisions in recent war crimes tribunals such as the ICTY, the ICTR, the ICC and so on, the *Geneva Convention* IV, the *Genocide Convention*, the *Hague Conventions on the Laws of War* and so forth.

Besides, this study shows that the intensive observations of the ICT-BD demonstrated again and again that the rape of women was used as a weapon by the Pakistani perpetrators and their local collaborators. From the perspectives of Bangladesh, ensuring legal justice is indeed the first step to be taken to redress the wrong done to the victims. The demand of rape victims to get social justice is widespread. This study would like to conclude that while legal justice has been examples, social justice is still demanded by the victims of 1971 Liberation War in Bangladesh. This study claims that there is ample scope to provide social justice to rape victims in various ways so that they can enjoy complete justice to some extent in their lifetime.

Abbreviations

AFRC	Armed Forces Revolutionary Council
BNWLA	Bangladesh National Women Lawyers' Association
DRC	Democratic Republic of the Congo
HCD	The High Court Division of the Supreme Court of Bangladesh
IAC	International Armed Conflict
ICC	International Criminal Court
ICC Statute	Statute of the International Criminal Court, 1998
ICHL	International Customary Humanitarian Law
ICT Act, 1973	International Crimes (Tribunals) Act, 1973
ICT-1	International Crimes Tribunal-1
ICT-2	International Crimes Tribunal-2
ICTA	International Crimes (Tribunals) Act, 1973
ICT-BD	International Crimes Tribunal of Bangladesh
ICTR	International Criminal Tribunal for Rwanda
ICTR Statute	Statute of the International Criminal Tribunal for Rwanda, 1994
ICTY	International Criminal Tribunal for the Former Yugoslavia
ICTY Statute	Statute of the International Criminal Tribunal for the Former Yugoslavia, 1993

IHL	International Humanitarian Law
NIAC	Non-International Armed Conflict
RUF	Revolutionary United Front
SCSL	Special Court for Sierra Leone
UN	The United Nations
WWII	World War II

1

Introduction

1.1 The Constitution of the People's Republic of Bangladesh is the supreme law of Bangladesh. It explicitly declares in its preamble that Bangladesh should establish a society where '... the rule of law, fundamental human rights and freedom, equality and justice, political, economic and social, will be secured for all citizens'.[1] The aspect of "equality and justice" is lucidly presented along with the social issue. Thus, our constitution emphasized the kind of justice which is "complete justice" and provides assurance of both legal and social justice. In this context, one notes that the issue of justice for rape victims of the 1971 Bangladesh War of Liberation still lacks comprehensive social and legal attention.

1.2 We all know that during war, rape is used as a deliberate military weapon.[2] Military personnel adopt rape as one of the

---

[1]   Please see Preamble and Part II of the *Constitution of the People's Republic of Bangladesh*.

[2]   Madeline Morris, 'By Force of Arms: Rape, War, and Military Culture' [1995-1996] 45 *Duke Law Journal* 651, 654; *See also* Laura Smith Spark, 'How Did Rape Become a Weapon of War?' *BBC News* (8 December 2004), available at <http://news.bbc.co.uk/2/hi/4078677.stm> accessed on 2 March 2017.

war tactics that includes not only a unique product formed out of a variety of physical factors but also as one of the moral and mental tactics deployed to defeat the enemy in action and battles.[3] Often the 'women bear more than their fair share of the burden' in almost all wars, being the subects of rape and other forms of sexual violence.[4] According to the *Explanatory Note of the Rome Statute of the International Criminal Court*, rape means invasion of the body of a person by conducts of the perpetrator that results in penetration in the sexual organ, or of the anal or genital opening of the victim, with any object or any other part of the body.[5]

1.3 At the time of war, army personnel conventionally attack women's sense of security and assault them in both physical and emotional senses.[6] By such means, perpetrators intend to humiliate the enemy men through the bodies of the women

---

[3]   Tactics, 'Department of the Navy Headquarters United States Marine Corps Washington' (30 July 1997) 3, available at <http://www.globalsecurity.org/military/library/policy/usmc/mcdp/1-3/mcdp1-3_fore.pdf> accessed on 3 March 2017; Robert Greene, *The 33 Strategies of War* (United States of America: Penguin Group and High Bridge Audio, 1st ed., 2006) 35.

[4]   Secretary-General Kofi Annan, 'United Nations Day for Women's Rights and International Peace' (6 March 2000), available at <http://www.un.org/press/en/2000/20000306.sgsm7325.doc.html> accessed on 16 March 2017; LaShawn R. Jefferson, 'In War as In Peace: Sexual Violence and Women's Status' *Human Rights Watch*, 1 (para. 3), available at <www.hrw.org/wr2k4/14.htm> accessed on 27 March 2017.

[5]   'The Statute of the International Criminal Court Protects against Sexual Crimes' *Smart Library on Globalization*, available at <https://clg.portalxm.com/library/keytext.cfm?keytext_id=204> accessed on 18 March 2017.

[6]   Nancy Farwell, 'War rape: New Conceptualizations and Responses' [2004] 19 (4) *Affilia* 389, 403.

in order to eventually weaken them mentally.[7] It should be mentioned here that although instances of the rape of women are mostly reported, rape of men also occur during war; nevertheless, such instances remain under-reported.[8] However, the scope of this paper is limited only to the context of the rape of women during the 1971 Bangladesh War of Liberation.

1.4 The history of the Bangladesh War of Liberation records the mass rape of Bangladeshi women by the Pakistan Army and their local collaborators (hereinafter referred to as "the perpetrators").[9]

---

[7]   Pascale R. Bos, 'Feminists Interpreting the Politics of Wartime Rape: Berlin 1945; Yugoslavia, 1992-1993' [2006] 31 (4) *The University of Chicago Press* 995, 1025; Reid-Cunningham and Allison Ruby, 'Rape as a Weapon of Genocide' [2008] 3 (3) *Genocide Studies and Prevention* 279, 296.

[8]   During the armed conflicts in Rwanda, Uganda, Burundi, Congo, several men were also raped who generally chose not to speak about such incidents; Lara Stemple, 'Male Rape and Human Rights' [2009] 60 (3) *Hastings Law Journal* 605, 619; Grace Natabaalo, 'Male Rape Survivors Fight Stigma in Uganda – Features' *Al Jazeera English* (30 April 2014), available at <http://www.aljazeera.com/indepth/features/2013/04/201341111517944475.html> accessed on 2 March 2017.

[9]   Local collaborators of the Pakistan Army included members of the Muslim League, Jamat-e-Islam, Neda-e-Islam and other Islamic groups and factions. They helped the Pakistan Army during the 1971 war of liberation, in identifying and killing millions of Bengalis directly involved in the war as *freedom fighters* or simply supporting them as civilians at the time of the liberation war. Local collaborators provided intelligence against the *freedom fighters*; abducted, arrested, and eventually killed many civilians with the help of *Pakistan Army* troops and party cadres in various army concentration camps and killings zones; burnt civilian houses and looted properties; kidnapped thousands of Bengali civilian women and trafficked them to various Pakistani military camps; raped and molested Bangladeshi women.

There is evidence that along with rape of Bangladeshi women, other forms of sexual violence such as sexual slavery, enforced prostitution, and forced pregnancy were also committed by the perpetrators.[10]

1.5 After about 40 years of our Liberation War, the matter of rape of the Bangladeshi women was brought under litigation to an extent in the International Crimes Tribunal of Bangladesh (ICT-BD). Both the *Syed Md. Qaiser*[11] and *A. T. M. Azharul Islam*[12] cases addressed the issues of war rape and reparation for the rape victims of Bangladesh. The other landmark cases which dealt with the issue of rape of women include *Delowar Hossain Sayeedi*,[13] *Abdul Quader Molla*,[14] *Moulana Abdul Kalam Azad*,[15] *Motiur Rahman Nizami*,[16] *Zahid Hossain Khokon*,[17] *Md. Forkan Mallik*,[18] *Mohibur Rahman alias Boro Mia, Mujibur Rahman alias Angur Mia and Md. Abdur Razzak and others*,[19] *Md. Sakhawat Hossain, Md.*

---

[10]   For further details, see, <http://muktadhara.net/page42.html> accessed on 23 March 2017.

[11]   *The Chief Prosecutor v. Syed Md. Qaiser*, ICTBD (II) Case No. 04 of 2013.

[12]   *The Chief Prosecutor v. A. T. M. Azharul Islam*, ICTBD (I) Case No. 05 of 2013.

[13]   *The Chief Prosecutor v. Delowar Hossain Sayeedi*, ICTBD (I) Case No. 01 of 2011.

[14]   *The Chief Prosecutor v. Abdul Quader Molla*, ICTBD (II) Case No. 02 of 2012.

[15]   *The Chief Prosecutor v. Moulana Abdul Kalam Azad*, ICTBD (II) Case No. 05 of 2012.

[16]   *The Chief Prosecutor v. Motiur Rahman Nizami*, ICTBD (I) Case No. 03 of 2011.

[17]   *The Chief Prosecutor v. Zahid Hossain Khokon @ M. A. Zahid @ Khokon Matubbar @ Khokon*, ICTBD (I) Case No. 04 of 2013.

[18]   *The Chief Prosecutor v. Md. Forkan Mallik @ Forkan*, ICTBD (II) Case No. 03 of 2014.

[19]   *The Chief Prosecutor v. Mohibur Rahman alias Boro Mia, Mujibur Rahman alias Angur Mia and Md. Abdur Razzak*, ICTBD (I) Case No. 03 of 2015.

Billal Hossain Biswas, Md. Lutfor, Md. Ibrahim Hossain, Sheikh Mohammad Mujibur Rahman, Md. A. Aziz Sardar, Abdul Aziz Sardar, Kazi Ohidul Islam, and Md. Abdul Khaleque Morol,[20] and *Md. Idris Ali Sardar and Md. Solaiman Mollah.*[21] In these cases, many witnesses[22] narrated their real time experiences in the form of their testimony before the ICT-BD. It may be mentioned here that some of the incidents were already reported in the form of oral history along with projection of certain wartime images and films. Along with dealings with the issue of legal justice for war rape victims, this research will endeavor to address various issues of social justice for victims of war rapes.

---

[20] *The Chief Prosecutor v. Md. Sakhawat Hossain, Md. Billal Hossain Biswas, Md. Lutfor, Md. Ibrahim Hossain, Sheikh Mohammad Mujibur Rahman, Md. A. Aziz Sardar, Abdul Aziz Sardar, Kazi Ohidul Islam, and Md. Abdul Khaleque Morol,* ICTBD (I) Case No. 04 of 2015.

[21] *The Chief Prosecutor v. Md. Idris Ali Sardar, and Md. Solaiman Mollah,* ICTBD (I) Case No. 06 of 2015.

[22] Both eye witnesses and part-eye witnesses.

2

Research Question

2.1 Some of the war criminals of the Liberation War of Bangladesh are being punished by the ICT-BD. It has been proved before the ICT-BD that the perpetrators were liable for committing or aiding/ abetting/ contributing/ facilitating/ conspiring to commit the offence of rape during the War of Liberation. Many war rape-victims and witnesses of such grave offences provided their testimonies before the Tribunals based on which the perpetrators were convicted and accordingly sentenced. Through this process, it is now popularly said by many that even though justice had been delayed, it was ultimately not denied.

2.2 However, a question remained unexplored as to whether *'legal justice'* essentially ensures *'social justice'* for the war rape victims in our country. It has been observed that war rape victims are still not socially recognized and/or respected; rather, they are considered as outcasts in our society. It has been mentioned earlier that about 0.5 million women were raped during the 1971 Liberation War of Bangladesh. It is a reality that many of these war rape victims died without even knowing that an attempt had been made to provide them with legal justice. Nevertheless, it is to be pointed out here that throughout the trial process, comparatively very few war rape victims were produced before the Court to give testimonies in particular cases. Other than these war rape victims-witnesses, there are many women in Bangladesh who are still unidentified. Unfortunately, nobody knows as to how justice is being perceived by them. Thus, it remains an unspoken narrative in our country in respect of how war rape victims actually perceive 'justice'.

2.3 Another question that arises in this regard is whether '*complete justice*' is being done in the course of ensuring legal justice to war rape victims. Apart from the question of social justice to them, it is to be mentioned here that the provision of *reparation* is not recognized under the *ICT Act*, 1973. Surprisingly, there is not a single monument in Bangladesh to commemorate the sacrifices of war rape victims. Even though in the case concerning *ATM Azharul Islam*,[23] it has been specified that the recognition of the war rape victims should be included in the school Text Books, this has not been done. Hence, it can be questioned as to how far 'justice' is being done to the war rape victims of Bangladesh only by the trial of war criminals?

2.4 This research would endeavor to get an account from the war rape victims and their families about the socio-legal aspects of the long-awaited justice. It may be mentioned that no systematic and/or comprehensive research has been conducted so far on this subject.

2.5 This research project also explores whether patriarchy is also an instrument used to commit sexual violence crimes. Patriarchy is the basic foundation of gender-based structural inequalities and unequal power relations between men and women. Patriarchy operates through ideologies and practices to create an unjust social structure, where women's subordination/inferior position and male domination and superiority are embedded.

---

[23] *A. T. M. Azharul Islam* (n 12).

Patriarchal social structures give birth to certain social norms and practices, religious doctrines, rituals, customs etc. which appear as 'normal', 'traditional' and therefore 'unquestionable' in the eyes of larger section of the population. Thus, division along gender lines creates a public-private dichotomy. From patriarchy directly derives patrilineal and patrilocal culture. Rigid patriarchal practices and women's subordination arguably give rise to gender discrimination and subject women to varied forms of violence, including rape, sexual torture etc. During war or armed conflicts, rape, sexual slavery and forced pregnancy are committed against women as a strategy of war for (a) destroying a nation/group/community, partially or wholly; and/or (b) planting the seeds of the male occupation-army personnel to the female of the subjugated nation/group/community; and/or (c) establishing control/domination of the male occupation-army personnel on the females of the subjugated nation/group/community.

2.6 This research work is of significance because even after a remarkable number of convictions of perpetrators by the ICT-BD and the Appellate Division of the Supreme Court of Bangladesh, it is still not clear how much justice is being done to victims in Bangladesh from socio-legal perspectives. We should not forget, '[n]ot only must Justice be done; it must also be seen to be done.'[24]

---

[24] *R v Sussex Justices, Ex parte McCarthy* [1924] 1 KB 256, [1923] All ER Rep 233.

3

Research Methodology

3.1 This research project mainly deployed a "legal research methodology" that included both "theoretical" and "empirical" approaches. "Legal research methodology" can be applied for various purposes such as interpretation or analysis of laws of a particular country, or to compare laws of different countries, or to know the consequences or effects of implementation of a law to ensure justice in society. It should be reiterated that this research work focuses on the issue of the impact of legal justice provided to war rape victims under the *International Crimes (Tribunals) Act 1973*. Hence, "legal research methodology" is the most relevant methodology needed to find out the effects of implementation of the said law to ensure "complete justice" to war rape victims in our society.

3.2 "Legal research methodology" involve two sources, namely, (a) legal sources, and (b) non-legal sources. "Legal sources" are used for the purpose of conducting mainly "theoretical research", whereas, "non-legal sources" are employed to conduct "empirical research". Firstly, "legal sources" entail both (i) the primary authority of law, and (ii) the secondary authority of law. "Primary authority of law" constitutes the law itself, and cases, statutes, regulations, codes *etc.* On the other hand, "secondary authority of law" includes commentary of non-Governmental bodies, reports, journals, legal treaties, encyclopedias, dictionaries *etc.* This research work is based on an analytical approach and critical appraisal of many statutes and judicial decisions of the following courts: International Crimes Tribunal – Bangladesh (ICT-BD), International Criminal Tribunal for the Former Yugoslavia (ICTY), International Criminal Tribunal for Rwanda (ICTR), International Criminal Court (ICC), Special Court for Sierra Leone (SCSL), and Nuremberg Trials etc. Again, relevant reports, journal articles and internet material were collected from various sources and considered in discussing the main issues here. It should be mentioned that "theoretical research" provides an understanding of how rape is used as a tactic and/or tool during war from national and international perspectives.

3.3 Secondly, "non-legal sources" are applied to gather supporting information for legal research on life styles, memories, experiences *etc.* of targeted respondents. For this purpose, "empirical approach" is used, which is, however, relatively a recent approach used in legal research. "Empirical research" is carried out by collecting and gathering data or information in relation to a particular research question. In short, "field survey research" is an essential element of this type of research in finding out the effect of legal decision on people and society as a whole.

3.4 The "field survey research" undertaken here was conducted using "qualitative data analysis" techniques. Such research involved using both standardized questionnaires and interviews to collect relevant data. The questions asked included both unstructured and structured questions. Unstructured questions were formed in such a way that respondents had the opportunity to provide responses in their own words. However, the structured questions gave respondents options to select an answer from a given set of choices.

3.5 For the purpose of the "field survey research" approach, the rape victims of the 1971 Liberation War of Bangladesh were interviewed. More specifically, "personal/face-to-face interviews" of war rape victims were conducted as a more personalized form of data collection method using the same research protocol as questionnaire surveys. The personal interviews were conducted in respondents' residence or other places convenient for interviewees.

3.6 To select respondents, the method of 'purposive selection' of war rape victims was invoked. To begin, the research team contacted the ICT-BD Investigation Agency and various District Command Councils of Freedom Fighters in each district of Bangladesh to gather information about the 1971 war rape victims as well as their contact addresses. From the information provided we prepared a long list of almost 1392 war rape victims of 1971 from 53 districts of the 8 Divisions of Bangladesh. Then the field researcher travelled to various districts to find out whether the listed 1392 war rape victims were interested in participating in our survey disclosing their identities. The field researcher then prepared a list of the 385 war rape victims who had consented to be interviewed disclosing their identity. Finally, the three-member team visited the listed 385 war rape victims to conduct survey. The research work has interviewed a total of 385 rape victims of 53 Districts of 8 Divisions of Bangladesh.

3.7 As far as research ethics is concerned, this research work ensured that the subjects of the field survey were aware that their participation in the study was voluntary. It was ensured that they felt they had the freedom to withdraw from the interview at any time without any unfavorable consequences, and they would not be harmed as a result of their participation or non-participation in this research project. The survey team also provided some information about this study to potential respondents before data collection to help them decide whether or not they wished to participate in the survey. The information included, *inter alia*, the identity of the survey researchers, the purpose and expected outcomes of the survey etc.

3.8 The overall analysis of the study was qualitative in nature and was contextualized based on a critical appraisal of many Statutes and judicial decisions of the Courts. The judicial decisions of the International Crimes Tribunal – Bangladesh (ICT-BD) was mainly focused on in the analysis. However, this research project also relied upon the judicial decisions of the International Tribunal for the Former Yugoslavia (ICTY), International Criminal Tribunal for Rwanda (ICTR), International Criminal Court (ICC), Special Court for Sierra Leone (SCSL), and Nuremberg Trials etc.

4

Historical Background

4.1 From rape and displacement to the denial of the right to food and medicines, women bear more than their fair share of the burden in any armed conflict situation.[25] In this context, over the years there has been growing international attention to the sexual violence committed during armed conflicts. Nevertheless, such crimes are routinely committed on a large scale against women in almost all wars.[26]

4.2 Bangladesh was born out of a 9-month long War of Liberation against the State of Pakistan in 1971. History records that there were mass killings of Bengali civilians and mass rape of Bangladeshi women by the Pakistan army and its local collaborators during the 1971 war. Very often the act of rape was followed by the act of killing of the rape victims. Besides there is evidence that other forms of sexual violence crimes were also committed by the Pakistan Army and its local collaborators against Bangladeshi women during 1971 war. These included sexual slavery, enforced prostitution, and forced pregnancy of Bangladeshi women.

---

[25]   Kofi Annan (n 4).

[26]   Jefferson (n 4).

4.3 Sexual Violence Crimes Committed against Bangladeshi Women during 1971 War

4.3.1 A number of sexual violence crimes were committed by the Pakistan Army and its local collaborators against Bangladeshi women during the 1971 War of Liberation. These included rape, sexual slavery, and forced pregnancy. A brief account of these three categories of sexual violence crimes committed against Bangladeshi women is given below:

4.3.2 Rape

4.3.2.1 During Bangladesh's War of Liberation against Pakistan in 1971, between 0.2 million and 0.4 million women were raped by solders and officers of the Pakistan Army and its local collaborators.[27] It may be stated that while the target was said to be largely Hindu women, Bangladeshi women, irrespective of religion, caste or class, came under the attack of the Pakistan Army and its local collaborators.[28] Indeed roughly 80% of rape victims were Bengali Muslims, while the rest were Hindus and Christians.[29] Also, the age of Bengali rape victims during 1971 war of liberation ranged between seven and seventy-five.[30]

---

[27] Shana Swiss and Joan E. Giller, 'Rape as a Crime of War: A Medical Perspective' [1993] 270 *Journal of the American Medical Association* 612, 612; Angela Debnath, 'The Bangladesh Genocide: The Plight of Women' in S Totten (ed), *Plight and Fate of Women During and Following Genocide* (New Brunswick: Transaction Publishers, 2009) 52.

[28] Kajalie Shehreen Islam, 'Healing the Hidden Wounds of War' 4 (12) *The Daily Star (Forum)*, Dhaka, December 2010.

[29] Kevin Gerard Neill, 'Duty, Honour, Rape: Sexual Assault against Women during War' [2000] 2 (1) *Journal of International Women's Studies,* 1, 2, available at <http://www.bridgew.edu/SoAS/jiws/nov00/duty.htm> accessed on 26 April 2017.

[30] Ibid.

4.3.2.2 The number of rape victims, released by the Government of Bangladesh after the war, amounted to only 0.2 million.[31] However, the War Inquiry Commission (popularly called the *Hamoodur Rahman Commission*), set up in 1971 by the President of Pakistan, claimed this number to be even much less.[32] The number dispute regarding the rape victims of 1971 should not be an issue in prosecuting such crimes. Generally, it is not at all possible to provide an exact number of rape victims in any society, be it during war or peace. The Bangladesh Government official data of rape victims was only a part of the total, since many rape victims of 1971 did not come forward to report or to receive government medical assistance fearing social ostracism.

4.3.2.3 Horrifying eye witness accounts of the plight of Bengali rape victims can be found in a number of international documents prepared by foreign correspondents and human rights workers who were in Bangladesh during 1971.[33] Also, there is literature

---

[31]   Anis Ahmed, 'Bangladesh 1971: War Crimes, Genocide and Crimes against Humanity- Operation Search Light: The Targets', conference paper presented at the Bangladesh Study Group programme at Kean University entitled *Bangladesh 1971: Addressing Claims of War Crimes, Genocide and Crimes against Humanity*, 18 October, 2009, 1, 9; *See also,* Susan Brownmiller, *Against Our Will: Men, Women and Rape* (New York: Ballantine Books, 1993) 133; Special Rapporteur on Violence Against Women in the November 1994 ECOSOC Report numbered E/CN.4/1995/42 presented at the fiftieth session of the Commission on Human Rights, at paragraph 271 (a); Ruth Seifert, 'War and Rape: Analytical Approaches', paper presented at the Women's International League for Peace and Freedom, Switzerland in April 1993, 1, 12.

[32]   *Hamoodur Rahman Commission Report*, Cabinet Secretariat, Government of Pakistan, Rawalpindi, 25 May 1974, para. 32.

[33]   Aubrey Menen, 'The Rape of Bangladesh', *The New York Times*, 23 July 1972, Column 2, paragraphs 8 and 9.

from the 1970s,[34] recent scholarship[35] and documentary films[36] based on eye witness accounts from within Bangladesh which shows that the Pakistan Army and its local collaborators committed rapes against Bangladeshi women and highlights the complexities of these violent encounters.[37] There is evidence too that some victims even lost their limbs, organs like breast, thigh, hip, were cut after the rape.[38] There is evidence that the Pakistan Army and its local collaborators killed young girls tearing their

---

[34] Germaine Greer, 'The Rape of the Bengali Women', *The Sunday Times*, April 9, 1972; S Brownmiller, Against *Our Will: Men, Women and Rape* (London: Secker & Warburg, 1975) 78-86.

[35] H H Rahman, *Bangladesher Shadhinota Juddho: Dolilpotro, Oshtom Khondo* (History of Bangladesh War of Independence: Documents, Vol-8) (Dhaka: Ministry of Information, 1984); Nilima Ibrahim, *Ami Birangona Bolchi* (This is the 'War-Heroine' Speaking), 2 Volumes (Dhaka: Jagriti, 1994-5); Meghna Guhathakurta, *Dhorshon Ekti Juddhaporadh* (Rape is a War Crime) (Dhaka: Bulletin of Ain-O-Shalish Kendra, 1996); Shaheen Akhtar, Suraiya Begum, Hameeda Hossain, Sultana Kamal, and Meghna Guhathakurta, (eds), *Narir Ekattor O Juddhoporoborti Koththo Kahini* (Oral History Accounts of Women's Experiences During 1971 and After the War) (Dhaka: Ain-O-Shalish-Kendro, 2001); Shahriar Kabir, *Tormenting Seventy One: An account of Pakistan Army's Atrocities during Bangladesh Liberation War of 1971* (Dhaka: Nirmul Committee, 2006).

[36] *Women and War*, directed by Tareque Masud and Catherine Masud, produced by Ain-O-Shalish-Kendra and Audiovision (2000); *Tahader Juddho* (Their War) directed by A Choudhury (2001).

[37] Nayanika Mookherjee, 'Bangladesh War of 1971: A Prescription for Reconciliation?' (2006) 41 (36) *Economic and Political Weekly* 3901; Nayanika Mookherjee, 'Skewing the History of Rape in 1971', 1 (2) *Daily Star Forum* (December 2006).

[38] Mofidul Hoque and Laurel Emilie Fletcher, *Colloquium on Accountability of Sexual Violence Crimes and Experiences of the International Tribunals* (Dhaka: Liberation War Museum, 2012) at p. 83.

thighs apart after raping them; they even publicly played football after cutting the breasts of the rape victims.[39]

4.3.3 Sexual Slavery

4.3.3.1 Many Bangladeshi women were not only raped during the 1971 War of Liberation, many were taken away by the Pakistan Army and its local collaborators and made to sex slaves of officers and soldiers for the duration of the war. These women, whether Hindu, Muslim or Christian, were captured either from private residences or educational institute premises (campus and girls' hostels).

4.3.3.2 Bangladeshi women, confided as sex slaves in military camps during the 1971 War of Liberation often received cruel, inhumane and degrading treatment. They were routinely tortured in horryfying ways. After these women tried to hang themselves with their clothing, their garments were taken away from them.[40] After they tried to strangle themselves with their long hair, they were shaved bald.[41]

4.3.4 Forced Pregnancy

4.3.4.1 Rape and sexual slavery committed by the Pakistan Army and its local collaborators during 1971 led to an estimated 0.025 million pregnancies among Bangladeshi women.[42] Since this data

---

[39] Information gathered from a personal interview with Monwara Begum, Investigation Officer, International Crimes Tribunal, Dhaka.

[40] Viggo Olsen and Jeanette Lockerbie, *Daktar: Diplomat in Bangladesh* (Chicago, USA, Moody Publishers, 1973).

[41] Ibid.

[42] Swiss & Giller (n 27).

is an official one, the actual number of pregnancies could have been much more than just 0.025 million. Many pregnancies were dealt or terminated without any kind of official medical support units, while many have remained unreported.[43]

4.3.4.2 In the aftermath of the war, the search for a solution by desperate Bangladeshi women who were victims of forced pregnancy led to the incidents of infanticide[44] and suicide. Authorities in Bangladesh have reported 300 suicides a week among pregnant women; however, many of these cases were not really suicides but unsuccessful attempts at self-induced abortion.[45]

4.3.4.3 Impregnating the Bangladeshi women was one of the war strategies adopted by the Pakistan Army and its local collaborators. Bangladeshi women, who were captivated as sex slaves, were found to have been released by the Pakistan Army and its local collaborators only when they became sure that those women were carrying the babies of Pakistani soldiers and were beyond the time limit set for abortion.[46] Even as many Pakistan forces surrendered in December 1971, some of the soldiers reportedly claimed that they were leaving their 'seed' behind in the women they had impregnated through mass rape.[47]

---

[43]   Personal interview with Maleka Begum, activist who worked directly with rape victims of 1971.

[44]   Associated Press, 'Killing of Babies Feared in Bengal', *The New York Times*, 5 March 1972.

[45]   Anthony Astrachan, 'U.N. Asked to Aid Bengali Abortions', *The Washington Post*, 22 March 1972 at column 2, paragraph 9.

[46]   'The World: East Pakistan: East Pakistan: Even the Skies Weep', *Time Magazine*, 25 October 1971.

[47]   Lisa Sharlach, '*Rape as Genocide: Bangladesh, the Former Yugoslavia, and Rwanda*' [2000] 22 (1) *New Political Science* 14.

5

Legal Implications Of Committing Rape During War

5.1 During medieval siege warfare, "rape" was used as a war tactic as a part of legal military techniques.[48] Later, through the development of the *Ordinances of War*, "death penalty" was imposed as a punishment to those responsible for adopting the rape of women during war.[49] Nevertheless, military men believed that all sorts of sexual violence including rape would be sources of inspiration to fight during war because they considered the same as rewards and means of relaxing(!).[50] With the passage of time, however, various legal instruments *i.e.* the Hague Conventions 1899 and 1907; the Four Geneva Conventions 1949; the Statute of the International Criminal Court (ICC Statute) 1998; the Statute of the International Criminal Tribunal for Rwanda (ICTR Statute) 1994; the Statute of the International Criminal Tribunal

---

[48] Patricia Viseur Sellers, 'Sexual Violence and Peremptory Norms: The Legal Value of Rape' [2002] 34 *Case Western Reserve Journal of International Law* 287, 288.

[49] Ibid.

[50] Kelly D. Askin, 'Prosecuting Wartime Rape and Other Gender-Related Crimes Under International Law: Extraordinary Advances, Enduring Obstacles' [2003] 21 *Berkeley Journal of International Law* 288, 296.

for the Former Yugoslavia (ICTY Statute) 1993; and even the International Crimes (Tribunals) Act (ICTA) 1973 *etc.* have been created prohibiting the use of rape as a tool of war.

5.2 Understanding the Concept of War Rape

5.2.1 World history is itself witness that the crime of rape has been in existence since ancient times. From then on, "war rape" has been labeled variously, *e.g.* collective rape, militarized rape, wartime rape, state-sponsored rape, martial rape *etc.*[51] This is sometimes termed as "genocidal rape";[52] however, there are differences in *mens rea* of the perpetrators to commit the same. Initially, rape had been theorized as a private concern of "disobedient" or "penurious" soldiers instead of considered as a matter of public concern.[53] However, due to its conventional consideration as a by-product of almost all armed conflicts, either "International Armed Conflict (IAC)" or "Non-International Armed Conflict (NIAC)" it is regarded as both an inexorable part of armed conflict and the effect of defeat in war.

5.2.2 Many States consider war rape from the perspective of morality through recognizing relevant customs and creating domestic laws.[54] However, the view that, the actual physical battery of soldiers would disrupt women's mental and physical

---

[51]   Elvan Isikozlu and Ananda S. Millard, 'Towards a Typology of Wartime Rape' Bonn International Center for Conversion 1, 21, available at <https://www.bicc.de/uploads/tx_bicctools/brief43.pdf> accessed on 18 February 2017.

[52]   Ibid.

[53]   Heaven Crawley, 'Engendering the State in Refugee Women's Claims for Asylum' in Susie Jacobs et al. eds., *States of Conflict: Gender, Violence and Resistance* (London: Zed Books, 2000) 87, 95.

[54]   William A. Schabas, *Genocide in International Law* (Cambridge: Cambridge University Press, 2000) 162.

integrity was historically ignored.[55] Some argued that male soldiers used rape during war to show their dominance to the men of opposite combatant community or group.[56]

5.2.3 In most cases, sexual violence crimes, including rape of women committed during armed conflicts remain unspoken. A written form of war rape was first found in ancient Greece.[57] Afterwards, during the 1938 Kristallnacht riots of Nazi Germany, certain written forms of "mass" war rape came into notice.[58] Subsequently, it was reported that Soviet soldiers raped more than 2 million German women at the end of the World War II (WWII).[59] Around the same period, the Japanese army also committed mass rape and abused thousands of Asian comfort women, mainly during the Nanking massacre.[60] In the 1971 War of Liberation of Bangladesh, the members of Pakistan Army, its auxiliary forces, and local collaborators raped approximately 0.2 million to 0.4 million women.[61] In recent times, the Report

---

[55]   Ibid.

[56]   Robert M. Hayden, 'Rape and Rape Avoidance in Ethno-National Conflicts: Sexual Violence in Liminalized States' [2000] 102 (1) *American Anthropologist* 27, 41.

[57]   H. Patricia Hynes, 'On the Battlefield of Women's Bodies: An Overview of the Harm of War to Women' [2004] 27 *Women's Studies International Forum* 431, 445.

[58]   D. Milillo, 'Rape as a Tactic of War: Social and Psychological Perspectives' [2006] 21 (2) *Journal of Women and Social Work* 196, 205.

[59]   Charles S. Maier, *The Unmiserable Past: History, Holocaust, and German National Identity* (Cambridge, MA: Harvard University Press, 1988) 321.

[60]   Shellie K. Park, 'Broken Silence: Redressing the Mass Rape and Sexual Enslavement of Asian Women by the Japanese Government in an Appropriate Forum' [2003] 3 *Asian Pacific Law and Policy Journal* 23, 24-5.

[61]   For further details, see, <http://muktadhara.net/page42.html> accessed on 23 March 2017.

of the Secretary General of the United Nations (UN) identified mass rape as having taken place during armed conflict in the Democratic Republic of the Congo (DRC), the Central African Republic, Iraq, Colombia, Somalia, South Sudan, the Sudan and the Syrian Arab Republic.[62]

5.2.4 In the 1971 Liberation War of Bangladesh, perpetrators of sexual violence against women regarded occupation of the Bangladeshi women's womb as one and the same as the occupation of the physical territory of Bangladesh. They intended to create fear among the people of Bangladesh and demoralize the spirit of the freedom fighters. Nonetheless, in the early 1990s, the international community was forced to rethink its policy regarding the use of rape as a tactic of war as well as a genocidal weapon, in the Hutu and Serbian regimes, in Rwanda and the former Yugoslavia.[63]

5.2.5 The experience of such warfare brought the "power element of the attack" into attention as the fundamental stimulus behind the adoption of such policy.[64] It was also realized that the purpose of using rape as a tactic of war is to "pollute and water down the bloodline" because the Serbs intended to destroy

---

[62] Report of the UN Secretary General on Conflict-Related Sexual Violence (23 March 2005) 1, 2, available at <http://www.securitycouncilreport.org/atf/cf/%7B65BFCF9B-6D27-4E9C-8CD3F6E4FF96FF9%7D/s_2015_203.pdf> accessed on 7 March 2017.

[63] These two countries are situated over five thousand miles apart; Jessica Kruger, 'A Comparative Analysis of Genocidal Rape in Rwanda and the Former Yugoslavia: Implications for the Future' [2011] *Master's Theses and Doctoral Dissertations Paper* 1, 3.

[64] Laurel Fletcher, Allyn Taylor, and Joan Fitzpatrick, 'Human Rights Violations against Women' [1994] 15 *Whittier Law Review* 319, 319; Kathleen Mahoney, *Rape as a War Crime and Crime against Humanity: Its Questionable Status, in Universal Human Rights?* (New York: Macmillan Press, 2000) 156 - 59.

both the soil and bloodlines.[65] It was probably thought that since women are well-regarded as mothers as well as defenders of their respective homes in many societies, the fact of their being raped would symbolize the ultimate victory of the military. From a broader perspective, it was seen that rape of a women caused embarrassment in an entire society where cultural and religious traditions and people's approach are used to disgrace victims of all sorts of sexual violence as was the case in Bangladesh, Sudan, Yugoslavia, and Rwanda.[66] Hence, it can be said that the inherent honour of the women in societies is the reason for using war rape of women as a war tactic which ultimately represents the criminality of such policy makers and executors.

5.3 Legal Inferences of Using Rape as a War Tactic

5.3.1 Under International Humanitarian Law (IHL), sexual violence crimes can take different forms. It does not only include rape but also, indecent assault, sexual slavery, enforced prostitution, forced pregnancy, enforced sterilization and/or any other form of sexual violence. Entering into a woman's body by force can be compared to an act of torture which ultimately causes physical pain, the loss of personal dignity and self-determination, and it is an attack on women's identity.[67] Many studies under the IHL have established that rape is an extreme act of violence perpetrated by the sexual means; it is an act or sexual expression

---

65   Amy E. Ray, 'The Shame of It: Gender-Based Terrorism in the Former Yugoslavia and the Failure of International Human Rights Law to Comprehend the Injuries' 46 [1997] 7 *American University Law Review* 93, 805-06.

66   Kelly D. Askin, 'Prosecuting Wartime Rape and Other Gender-Related Crimes under International Law: Extraordinary Advances, Enduring Obstacles' [2003] 21 *Berkeley Journal of International Law* 288, 289-93.

67   Ibid.

of aggression itself. Kelly Askin, the Director of the International Criminal Justice Institute (ICJI), opines that "there is increasing evidence that sexual violence has now reached the level of a *jus cogens* norm."[68]

5.3.2 In order to be focused on only war rape, Rule 93 of the International Customary Humanitarian Law (ICHL) can be referred.[69] This particular Rule depicts that '[r]ape and other forms of sexual violence are prohibited'.[70] The 1907 Hague Convention Respecting the Laws and Customs of War on Land indicates what type of behavior is acceptable in the course of a war. This Convention did not explicitly specify any prohibition of war rape; however, it has been progressively interpreted to bar rape in the framework of war. From the perspective of broader interpretation, Article 46 of the Hague Convention obliges combatants to respect the "family honour and rights, [and] the lives of persons" during war.[71] Therefore, it can be inferred that this *Convention* also prohibits rape.

5.3.3 Under the purview of common Article 3 of the 1949 *Four Geneva Conventions*, brutality to life and person by the way of torture, *inter alia*, which causes outrage upon personal dignity is absolutely prohibited against the *hors de combat* who do not take part in hostilities during armed conflict. Similarly, Article 27 of the 1949 *Fourth Geneva Convention*, related to the protection of civilian persons in times of war, explicitly prohibits wartime rape

---

[68] Id.

[69] *International Customary Humanitarian Law* (ICHL) as codified by the International Committee of the Red Cross (ICRC), available at <https://ihl-databases.icrc.org/customary-ihl/eng/docs/v1_rul_rule93> accessed on 8 March 2017.

[70] Ibid, Rule 93.

[71] C. P. M. Cleiren and M. E. M. Tijssen, 'Rape and Other Forms of Sexual Assault in the Armed Conflict in the Former Yugoslavia: Legal Procedural, and Evidentiary Issues, in the Prosecution of International Crimes' [1994] *Criminal Law Forum* 280, 287.

and enforced prostitution. The second paragraph of Article 27 reads: '[w]omen shall be especially protected against any attack on their honour, in particular against rape, enforced prostitution, or any form of indecent assault.'[72] These prohibitions were reinforced by the 1977 Additional Protocols to the Geneva Conventions.[73]

5.3.4 In 1974, the UN General Assembly adopted the Declaration on the Protection of Women and Children in Emergency and Armed Conflict.[74] This Declaration urges states to ensure protection for women in compliance with international laws, including the *Geneva Conventions*.[75] Surprisingly, this declaration does not refer explicitly to women's vulnerability to sexual violence during armed conflict, even though this was evident from the report of the Special Rapporteur on violence against women that rape was committed against Bangladeshi women on a large scale during the 1971 war.[76] However, from the *travaux préparatoires* of this *Declaration* it has been easy to perceive that the role of women as "mothers and care-givers" were taken into

---

[72] Article 27 of the Fourth Geneva Convention, 1949; For a discussion of the four Geneva Conventions, along with the State parties, see the website of the International Committee of the Red Cross (ICRC), available at <http://www.icrc.org/Web/Eng/siteeng0.nsf/html/genevaconventions> accessed on 1 March 2017.

[73] In the *Nicaragua* case, the International Court of Justice (ICJ) concluded that the Conventions' principles amount to "elementary considerations of humanity" that cannot be breached in war, regardless of whether the conflict is international or national in nature; Cleiren and Tijssen (n 67).

[74] *The United Nations Declaration on the Protection of Women and Children in Emergency and Armed Conflict*, General Assembly Resolution 3318 (XXIX) (14 December 1974) preamble, paras. 9 and 3.

[75] Ibid.

[76] *Id*, para. 271 (a).

consideration as regards the situation of women during armed conflict.[77]

5.3.5 After a certain period of time, the ICC Statute was adopted which gives the International Criminal Court (ICC) jurisdiction over genocide, crimes against humanity, and war crimes. Although both men and women can be victims of most of these crimes, some of them, such as forced pregnancy, can be committed only against women. Articles 7 and 8 of the *ICC Statute* included rape, sexual slavery, enforced prostitution, forced pregnancy, enforced sterilization, and other forms of sexual violence, both as explicit crimes against humanity[78] and implicitly, war crimes.[79]

5.3.6 In 1998, the ICTR made a landmark decision in the *Jean-Paul Akayesu* case that considered "rape as genocide" under the international law even though the concerned accused was convicted for committing rape as a "crime against humanity".[80] Specifically, this case recognized rape as a "crime of genocide" for the first time on the ground that rape causes "serious bodily or mental harm" to victims belonging to any of the four indentifiable groups (*i.e.* national, racial, ethnical, and religious) as long as the same is committed with the "specific intent to destroy such group in whole or in part".[81]

---

[77] *Id*, para. 4.

[78] The *ICC Statute* 1998, Article 7 (1) (g) and Article 7(2) (c), (e) and (f).

[79] Ibid; Article 8 (b) (xxi) and (b) (xxii).

[80] *The Prosecutor v. Jean-Paul Akayesu*, ICTR-96-4-T (Trial Chamber), 2 September 1998.

[81] Ibid, at paras. 688 and 731; *The Prosecutor v. Sylvestre Gacumbitsi*, ICTR-2001-64 (Trial Chamber), 17 June 2004, para. 292; *The Prosecutor v. Blagojevic and Jokic*, IT-02-60-T (Trial Chamber), 17 January 2005, para. 646; *The Prosecutor v. Radislav Krstic*, IT-98-33-T (Trial Chamber), 2 August 2001, para. 513; *The Prosecutor v. Milomir Stakic*, IT-97-24-T (Trial Chamber), 31 July 2003, para. 516; *The Prosecutor v. Radoslav Brdjanin*, IT-99-36-T (Trial Chamber), 1 September 2004, para. 690.

5.3.7 In the same year, sexual violence involving rape was recognized for the first time as a "war crime" in the *Furundzija* case by ICTY pointing out that *a* single rape may constitute a war crime.[82] Likewise, in 2001, in the *Dragoljub Kunarak, Radomir Kovak and Zoran Vukovic* case, *ICTY concluded that even a single rape may constitute a "crime against humanity".*[83] Sexual violence was held to fall under "crimes against humanity" through various means; for example, as enslavement,[84] as sexual slavery,[85] as persecution,[86] as forced marriage[87] or even, as torture[88].

5.3.8 On 19 June 2008, a 15-Member UN Security Council unanimously adopted *Resolution 1820 (2008)* on 'Sexual Violence against Civilians in Conflict'. The *Resolution* condemns the use of rape and other forms of sexual violence in conflict situations, stating that rape can constitute a "war crime", a "crime against humanity", or a constitutive act with respect to "genocide".[89]

---

82   *The Prosecutor v. Furundzija*, IT-95-17/1-T (Trial Chamber), 10 December 1998.

83   *The Prosecutor v. Dragoljub Kunarak, Radomir Kovak and Zoran Vukovic, IT-96-23-T and 23/1-T (Trial Chamber), 22 February 2001;* Christopher Scott Maravilla, 'Rape as a War Crime: The Implication of the International Criminal Tribunal for the Former Yugoslavia's Decision in *Prosecutor v. Kunarac Kovac and Vukovic* on International Humanitarian Law' [2001] 13 *Florida Journal of International Law* 321, 322-23; *A. T. M. Azharul Islam Case* (n 11), at page 140 at para. 264.

84   Ibid.

85   *The Prosecutor v. Sesay et. al.*, SCSL-04-15-T (Trial Chamber), 2 March 2009.

86   *The Prosecutor v. Kvocka*, IT-98-30/I-T (Trial Chamber), 2 November 2001.

87   *The Prosecutor v. Brima et. al.*, SCSL-04-16-T (Trial Chamber), 20 June 2007 and SCSL-2004-16-A (Appeals Chamber), 22 February 2008 ('*AFRC*' Case).

88   *The Prosecutor v. Semanza*, ICTR-97-20 (Trial Chamber), 15 May 2003.

89   Paragraph 5 of the Preamble of the Resolution 1820 (2008)

6

Patriarchy And War As Instruments
Of Sexual Violence Crime

6.1 Patriarchy is an anthropological term and has been defined by Sarah Blaffer Hrdy as 'an ideology that focused on both the chastity of women and the perpetuation and augmentation of male lineages undercut the long-standing priority of putting children's well-being first'.[90] For Hrdy, when people started to become agrarian and urban, patriarchy entered into the human society of the world.[91] Likewise, Wendy Wood and Alice Eagly contend that when human beings were hunter-gatherers, patriarchy was not in existence for a long period of human history.[92] Wood and

---

adopted by the Security Council at its 5916th Meeting on 19 June 2008.

[90] Carol Gilligan, *The Birth of Pleasure* (New York: Alfred A. Knopf, 2002) 4 – 5; *See also*, Arundhati Roy, *The God of Small Things* (New York: Harper Perennial, 1998) 6; Frans de Wall, *The Age of Empathy: Nature's Lessons for a Kinder Society* (New York: Harmony Books, 2009) 7.

[91] Ibid.

[92] Wendy Wood and Alice H Eagly, 'A Cross-Cultural Analysis of the Behavior of Women and Men: Implications for the Origins of Sex Differences' [2002] 128 *Psychological Bulletin* 699, 704.

Eagly, however, pointed at the relatively late development of the concept of patriarchy and introduced a bio-social model of 'the interactive relations between the physical attributes of men and women and the social contexts in which they live'.[93]

6.2 Again, considering the development of patriarchy, Hrdy argues that '[m]en are now pulled into closer patriarchal relationships with other men for purposes of politics and war, with the associated consequences for the role of women.'[94] Sarah Lemer puts it forward as to 'how myth, religion, science and politics - all features of high patriarchal cultures - unite in an ideological attack on what must have been obvious even then, the facts of human relationality.'[95] She notes that the 'patriarchal demand is control of women's sexuality which included an aggressive war on women's free sexuality as an expression of their own convictions ...'[96]

6.3 As regards war rape and patriarchy, the ICTY very lucidly observed in 2001 in the case concerning *Krstic*[97] that the 'community of Bosnian Muslims from the Srebrenica area was 'patriarchal', and that patriarchy was instrumental in the commissioning of genocide by committing rape.'[98] Moreover, world history is itself a witness of the fact that the crime of rape

---

93 Ibid, 701.

94 Sarah Blaffer Hrdy, *Mothers and Others: The Evolutionary Origins of Mutual Understanding* (Belknap Press: Harvard University Press, 2009) 204 - 238, 239 - 243, 261 - 265, 287 - 290.

95 Ruth Rosen, *The World Split Open: How the Modern Women's Movement Changed America* (New York and London: Penguin, 2001) 107, 116, 122, 126, 129.

96 Brownmiller (n 34); David P. Bryden and Sonja Lengnick, 'Rape in the Criminal Justice System' [1997] 87 *Journal of Criminal Law & Criminology* 1194, 1195 - 1198.

97 IT-98-33-T (Trial Chamber), 02 August 2001.

98 Doris E. Buss, 'Knowing Women: Translating Patriarchy in International Criminal Law' [2014] 23 *Social & Legal Studies* 73-74, 92; David P. Bryden and Erica Madore, 'Patriarchy, Sexual

has been in existence since ancient periods of wartime where patriarchy was found to be an instrument of sexual violence.

6.4 Initially, rape was theorized as a private concern of "disobedient" or "penurious" soldiers instead of as a matter of public concern.[99] However, due to its conventional acceptance as a by-product of almost all armed conflicts, either "International Armed Conflict (IAC)" or "Non-International Armed Conflict (NIAC)", rape was regarded as both the inexorable part of armed conflict and an effect of defeat in war.

6.5 Many states have started to consider war rape from the perspective of morality factoring in relevant customs and re-enacting domestic laws.[100] However, the view that, the actual physical batter of the soldiers would disrupt women's mental and physical integrity had been historically ignored.[101] Some have argued that male soldiers used to rape women during war to assert their superiority and show their power to the men of such women's communities or groups.[102] Accordingly, the philosopher Claudia Card has clearly pointed out that '[the war rape is a] cross-cultural language of male domination'.[103] The policy of war rape was adopted mostly to undermine the political, cultural, and national solidarity of the targeted people with a view to changing the identity of that particular group or community.[104]

Freedom, and Gender Equality as Causes of Rape' [2016] 13 *Ohio State University Journal of Criminal Law* 299, 345.

[99] Heaven Crawley, 'Engendering the State in Refugee Women's Claims for Asylum' in Susie Jacobs et al. eds., *States of Conflict: Gender, Violence and Resistance* (London: Zed Books, 2000) 87, 95.

[100] William A. Schabas, *Genocide in International Law* (Cambridge: Cambridge University Press, 2000) 162.

[101] Ibid.

[102] Robert M. Hayden (n 56).

[103] Claudia Card, 'Rape as a Weapon of War' [1996] 11 (4) *Hypatia* 5, 18.

[104] Cunningham and Ruby (n 7).

Nevertheless, and reflecting on this ignorance of the matter of using rape as a "tool of war", a leading commentator December Green, has opined that rape is 'one of the most pernicious and least understood aspects of war.'[105]

6.6 Concerning the contexts of rape that happened during the Liberation War of Bangladesh and the trials of the perpetrators, in the *Md. Idris Ali Sardar and others case*[106] the ICT-BD noted:

> 'Rape is an offence which is more than murder. The trauma the victim sustains kills her endlessly. Bodily harm the victim sustains gets healed but psychological and mental harms are never erased. Rape or sexual violence causes serious bodily and mental harm not to the victim only but to her family, the society and the community she belongs.'[107]

6.7 Considering these factors, the Tribunal found that committing rape and other sexual violence upon Hindu women captives in this particular case portrays the genocidal intent of the perpetrators to destroy Hindu religious group(s).[108] The Tribunal also opined that rape was used as a "tool of destruction", and a "tool of genocide" of the targeted group(s) causing both physical and psychological annihilation of Bengali Hindu women.[109] Besides, as regards the bodily and mental harm of women who suffered from instance of such genocidal rape, the Tribunal stipulated that since '[f]amily honour and religious group identity are enmeshed with female chastity [,] [w]omen who endured the genocidal rape

---

105 December Green, *Gender Violence in Africa: African Women's Response* (New York: St. Martin's Press, 1999) 51, 241.

106 *Md. Idris Ali Sardar and Others*, ICTBD (I) Case No. 06 of 2015.

107 Ibid, para. 335.

108 *Id*, para. 332.

109 *Id*, para. 343.

had to cope not only with their physical injuries and trauma they sustained, but with a society and community they belong.'[110]

6.8 In its verdict on the *Md. Moslem Prodhan and Syed Md. Hossian* case of the ICT-BD, the Tribunal also viewed rape as a "tool of genocide".[111] Concerning the course of destruction, the Tribunal pointed out the 'coercive and horrific situation' created by the perpetrators committing rape and other sexual violence upon Hindu religious women in targeted localities.[112] Like the *Md. Idris Ali Sardar and others* case, the Tribunal noted in this case as well that the acts of rape not only caused bodily and mental harm to women but also to their families and communities which ultimately lead it to conclude that the perpetrators intended to destroy Hindu religious groups, either wholly or partly.[113] From the above description, it is therefore clear that the perpetrators used rape of Bangladeshi women not only as a "weapon of war" but also as a "tool of genocide".

6.9 As an end note to this part, it should be mentioned that in case of the war in Bosnia and Herzegovina in the 1990s, it was reported by the Williams Institute that some 0.003 million men and boys were raped but their stories remain untold in Bosnia's macho culture.[114] Similarly, in the case of the Liberation War of Bangladesh, such cases have been a part of oral history that many men were also raped by the perpetrators but any data or report in this regard is yet to be explored.

---

[110] *Id*, para. 355.

[111] *Md. Moslem Prodhan and another*, ICTBD (I) Case No. 01 of 2016, para. 420.

[112] Ibid, para. 394.

[113] *Id*.

[114] Maja Garaca Djurdjevic and Banja Luka, 'Wartime Rapes of Men Remains Taboo in Bosnia' [2017] *Balkan Transitional Justice*, available at <http://www.balkaninsight.com/en/article/male-victims-of-war-related-sexual-abuse-shunned-in-bosnia-05-18-2017-1/1455/4> accessed on 25 March 2017.

7

Understanding Justice: Global Perspectives

7.1 The demand for justice is not confined within the wall of only "justice", rather, it has to be extended to meet the demand for "complete justice" in our time. We hear from here and there that injustices are committed in many places around the world. However, what really is justice? We often ask this question to others and sometimes even to ourselves. We do not always get a convincing explanation in this regard.

7.2 Preliminary Concept of Justice

7.2.1 Justice is a universal and absolute concept which is codified by laws, principles, religions, cultures, traditions *etc.*[115] With the passage of time, many justice principles and theories have emerged but a unitary concept of justice is yet to be developed. Scholars have attempted to divide the concept of justice into different categories such as social, legal, criminal,

---

[115] Max Travers, 'Understanding Comparison Research Foundation: An Interpretive Perspective,' [2008] 18 *International Criminal Justice Review* 389, 395; Michael Head, 'Law, Social Change and Social Justice,' [2001] 5 *University of Western Sydney Law* 3, 17.

civil, global, commutative, distributive, open, organizational, poetic, restorative, retributive, spatial, occupational justice, and absolute justice.[116]

7.2.2 This research work is however concerned about socio-legal aspects of justice, mainly for the 1971 war rape victims in Bangladesh. Thus, the connection between social justice in relationship to legal justice will be explored in this part referring to prevalent principles and theories of justice. To determine what social justice means it is necessary to define justice at the very beginning. Thus, this part firstly defines justice, and then delineates social justice with regard to legal justice and then attempts a critical evaluation of such concepts.

7.3 Defining Justice

7.3.1 Graveson defined 'justice is to a great extent a legal reflection of ethical and moral values conditioned by time, place and circumstances, much as the concept of reasonableness in common law is a reflection of contemporary social values.'[117] This definition may be more appropriate for the present research. Nevertheless, there are number of remarkable notions and theories of justice that have evolved from the ancient period of time. At a very early period of time, the Ancient Greek philosopher Plato declared that 'justice is that justice is the having and doing of what is one's own.'[118] This view-point of Plato was applicable

---

[116] Robert Wablder, 'The Concept of Justice and the Quest for a Perfectly Just Society' [1966-67] 115 *University of Pennsylvania Law Review* 1, 13; Alice Erh-Soon Tay, 'The Concept of Justice as Social Regulator in Law, Politics, Economics and Culture' [1981] *Bulletin of the Australian Society of Legal Philosophy* 2, 9-10.

[117] Barbara A. Hudson, *Understanding Justice* (Open University Press: United Kingdom, 1996) 192, 221.

[118] R. W. Carlyle & A. J. Carlyle, *A History of Mediaeval History in the*

both at the individual level and at the universal level.[119] With the passage of time, many theories have emerged and gradually been developed by theorists like John Locke, John Stuart Mill, John Rawls, Robert Nozick, Immanuel Kant and C. S. Lewis and so on.

7.3.2 The advocates of the "command theory" believe that justice is nothing but an authoritative command of God.[120] On questions of morality and justice, Plato criticized this theory by asking as to '[i]s what is morally good commanded by God because it is morally good, or is it morally good because it is commanded by God?'[121] In other words, the former question implies that the existence of morality is more pertinent than the question of the God whereas the later question suggests the arbitrariness of justice. In this regard, Immanuel Kant responded that when objective morality exists, God also exists and *vice versa*.[122] Hence,

---

West: The Theory of the King and Justice (Barnes & Noble: New York, 3rd ed., 1903) 219, 226.

[119] Ibid; Anton-Hermann Chroust and David L. Osborn, 'Aristotle's Conception of Justice,' [1942] 17 (2) *Notre Dame Law Review* 129, 152-3; Robert Wablder, 'The Concept of Justice and the Quest for a Perfectly Just Society' [1966 - 1997] *University of Pennsylvania Law Review* 1, 27.

[120] Robert Rubinson, 'A Theory of Access to Justice,' [2004-5] 29 *Journal of the Legal Profession* 89, 103; *See also*, Eugene Kamenka and Alice Erh-Soon Tay, 'Marxist Ideology, Communist Reality, and the Concept of Criminal Justice' [1987] 6 *Criminal Justice Ethics* 3, 16.

[121] R. W. Carlyle and A. J. Carlyle, *A History of Mediaeval History in the West: The Theory of the King and Justice* (New York: Barnes & Noble, 3rd ed., 1903) 219, 227 - 228; Anton-Hermann Chroust and David L. Osborn, 'Aristotle's Conception of Justice' [1942] 17(2) *Notre Dame Law Review* 129, 159.

[122] Kieran McEvoy, 'Beyond Legalism: Towards a Thicker Understanding of Transitional Justice,' [2007] 34 *Journal of Law & Society* 411, 424; *See also*, Samuel Taylor Morison, 'A Hayekian Theory of Social Justice' [2005] 1 *NYU Journal of Law & Liberty* 225, 232.

justice is simply a reflection of morality that comes from the command of the God.

7.3.3 From the "natural law" theory perspectives, during the 17th century, John Locke opined that justice is itself a part of natural law and it is a result of an action and/or choice.[123] Interestingly, seen from the perspective of the third principle of the "Laws of Motion of Newton", justice is what an individual, being the offender and victim, deserves, based on his/her action(s) and harm caused respectively as an equal and opposite reaction of such action.[124] Next, during the 19th century, John Stuart Mill, a utilitarian thinker, explained the sources of the concept of justice and stated that it was derived from standards of rightness as well as consequentialism.[125] Whether a principle of justice is regarded as the most accepted one depends on its consequence measured by the extent of well-being it contributes to society.

7.3.4 Another theory of justice is the "distributive justice" theory which includes, *inter alia*, wealth, power, opportunities, respect distributed to the human beings, members of a society, a nation in the forms of social justice, fairness, property rights, maximization of welfare *etc.*[126] The notion of social justice will be

---

[123] Marius Van Staden, 'Towards a South African Understanding of Social Justice: The International Labour Organisation Perspective,' [2012] *Journal of South African Law* 91, 93; Bradley C. Bobertz, 'Toward a Better Understanding of Intergenerational Justice,' [1987] 36 *Buffalo Law Review* 165, 167.

[124] John Braithwaite, 'Restorative Justice and Social Justice,' [2000] 63 *Saskatchewan Law Review* 185, 188-9; Anton-Hermann Chroust and David L. Osborn, 'Aristotle's Conception of Justice' [1942] 17(2) *Notre Dame Law Review* 129, 131.

[125] Ibid, Braithwaite, 190; *See also*, Matthew Kramer, 'The Deferral of Nature in Hume's Theory of Justice' [1989] 2 *Canadian Journal of Law & Jurisprudence* 139, 151.

[126] Leroy Marceau, 'A Descriptive Theory of Justice,' [1944-6] 6 *Louisiana Law Review* 350, 363; *See also*, George Mousourakis,

explored in the following part although it is important to mention at the outset that according to John Rawls 'distributive justice, is a form of fairness' with the connection of social contract theory.[127] Significantly, social justice is a branch of the virtue of justice which advises us to use our best efforts to ensure a more just justice to people. What's more, Robert Nozick notes that distributive justice is property rights-based justice which takes advantage of the overall resources of an economic system.[128]

7.3.5 Other popular theories of justice are the "retributive justice" theory and the "restorative justice or reparative justice" theory. The former theory is concerned with providing appropriate punishment to offenders for committing crimes, whereas the later one concentrates on the needs of victims and offenders considering what is for their good.[129]

7.3.6 Together with the scholars' views and theories of justice, from time to time certain stages have been perceived in the evolution of the idea of justice. For example, the ancient idea was that justice is an essential device for keeping peace in society.[130] 'Whatever served to avert private vengeance and prevent private war was an instrument of justice.'[131] At one time, many laws existed as a body of rules and regulations based on which the

---

'Understanding and Implementing Restorative Justice,' [2003-4] 11 *Tilburg Foreign L. Rev.* 626, 657.

[127] Ibid, Mousourakis, 632; Roger Wertheimer, 'Understanding Retribution' [1983] 2 *Criminal Justice Ethics* 19, 26-27.

[128] *Id; See also,* Julius Stone, 'A Critique of Pound's Theory of Justice,' [1934-5] 20 *Iowa Law Review* 531, 536.

[129] *Id;* Henry M. Gottlieb, 'Legal Rights and Social Justice' [1932-1933] 2 *University of Detroit Journal of Urban Law* 28, 31.

[130] Notes and Comments, 'Social Justice and Legal Justice,' [1912] 75 *Central Law Journal* 455, 456; Leroy Marceau, 'A Descriptive Theory of Justice' [1944 - 1946] 6 *Louisiana Law Review* 350, 350.

[131] Ibid.

disputes were resolved nonbelligerenly.[132] As the outcome of the justice process, injured persons were given a 'substitute for revenge'.[133] Nonetheless, in modern justice system, the offenders are compelled to provide "compensation" to the injured for the desire to be avenged.[134] In Roman law, such compensation was given under the head of "insult".[135] The Salic law used to impose "double compensation" to the offenders to accustom to right their own wrongs for generations to adjust the same.[136]

7.3.7 Greek philosophy and Roman law regarded the "idea of justice" as a device for the preservation of the social *status quo*.[137] In other words, Plato explained it saying that, 'in an ideal state, "every member of the community must be assigned to the class for which he proves himself."'[138] In this context, Roman legal genius added that such social *status quo* has to be upheld by the concerned authority of a State by defining and protecting the interests and powers of the actions of individuals.[139] Justinian principle of living honourably, avoiding causing injury to others, as well as giving every man his/her due-express is considered a

---

[132] Dean J. Spader, 'Megatrends in Criminal Justice Theory' [1985 – 1986] 13 *American Journal of Criminal Justice* 157, 170.

[133] Ibid, 171; *See also*, Thomas Obel Hansen, 'Transitional Justice: Toward a Differentiated Theory' [2011] 13 *Oregon Review of International Law* 1, 14.

[134] Robert Rubinson, 'A Theory of Access to Justice' [2004 – 2005] 29 *Journal of the Legal Profession* 89, 93.

[135] Ibid; *See also*, Sidney M. Schreiber, 'Justice Pashman's Jurisprudential Theory of Justice: Justice' [1982- 1983] 35 *Rutgers Law Review* 207, 212.

[136] Notes and Comments, 'Social Justice and Legal Justice,' [1912] 75 *Central Law Journal* 455, 455 - 556.

[137] Ibid, 456.

[138] *Id*; Dan W. Brockt, 'The Theory of Justice' [1972 – 1973] 40 *University of Chicago Law Review* 486, 490.

[139] Rex Martin, 'Rawls's New Theory of Justice' [1993 – 1994] 69 *Chicago-Kent Law Review* 737, 752.

seminal idea of justice.[140] In addition, from the orthodox view of Aristotle, it can be said that justice means the perspectives of the just man 'who is bound to act justly.'[141] It should be mentioned here that the idea of justice is not limited to the "duty to act justly", rather, it is extended to the "demand for just treatment".[142]

7.3.8 Even in the anterior period of time, the objective of such justice was to restore the original position i.e. preferring the form of "individual justice" instead of "social justice".[143] Such kind of justice was not categorized "social justice" on the ground that the claims were not conceived against all members of society, rather, claims were considered more individualistic.[144] On the other hand, Aristotle explained,

> It is thought that justice is equality, and so it is, though not for everybody but only for those who are equals; and it is thought that inequality is just, for so indeed it is, though not for everybody, but for those who are unequal.[145]

---

[140]   Ibid, 457; *See also*, Robert E. Rodes, 'Social Justice and Liberation' [1995 – 1996] 71 *Notre Dame Law Review* 619, 642.

[141]   A. M. Honore, 'Social Justice,' [1961-62] 8 *McGill Law Journal* 77, 79-80; Anton-Hermann Chroust and David L. Osborn, 'Aristotle's Conception of Justice' [1992] 17 (2) *Notre Dame Law Review* 129, 130 – 131.

[142]   Ibid.

[143]   *Id*, 81-82; *See also*, Marius Van Staden, 'Towards a South African understanding of social justice: The International Labour Organisation Perspective' [2012] *Journal of South African Law* 91, 92.

[144]   Ibid, 83.

[145]   Robert Wablder, 'The Concept of Justice and the Quest for a Perfectly Just Society' [1966-67] 115 *University of Pennsylvania Law Review* 1, 2.

7.3.9 Given the perspectives presented above, it is clear that sometimes the demand for "absolute justice" creates difficulties in questions of justice as mysterious even though the very concept itself may sound noble.

7.4 The Notion of Social Justice

7.4.1 Representing a classical Western traditional view, Thomas Aquinas defined justice as a virtue which is a character in a human being's willpower to act rightly.[146] Corresponding to the previous discussion on the concept of justice, Thomas opines that "commutative" and "distributive" are two forms of justice.[147] It should be mentioned that the very idea of "distributive justice" is similar to the up-to-date use of "social justice".[148] It should be noted that every, so often, distributive justice and social justice are considered as separate from the standpoint that the former one is determined geometrically as per the common good, while later one is resolute arithmetically demanding for absolute justice.[149]

7.4.2 However, John Augustine Ryan emphasis both the commutative and distributive justice to define social justice.[150] He suggested that the idea of social justice broadened understanding of its concept.[151] In this regard, Professor Conor Gearty has argued

---

[146] John Wehrly, 'Conservative Social Justice' [2009] 3 *University of St. Thomas Journal of Law & Public Policy* 113, 113; Eric Rakowski, 'On a New Theory of Justice' [1994] 82 *California Law Review* 231, 239.

[147] Ibid, 113 - 4.

[148] *Id*; D. J. Bentley, 'John Rawls: A Theory of Justice' [1972 – 1973] 121 *University of Pennsylvania Law Review* 1070, 1103.

[149] Ibid, 114; *See also*, Barbara A. Hudson, 'Understanding Justice' [1998] 18 *Critical Social Policy* 125, 131.

[150] Harlan R. Beckley, 'The Legacy of John A. Ryan's Theory of Justice' [1988] 33 *American Journal of Juris* 61, 76.

[151] Ibid.

that 'Ryan's early use of the concepts of "human welfare" and the "common good" in determining his understanding of "social justice" and its influence upon his conception' was not sound.[152] Although, Ryan did not define the concept of social justice, he has very lucidly stated that "social justice" is a combination of "legal justice", involving obligation of the individuals along with distributive justice.[153]

7.4.3 Corresponding to Ryan's view, throughout the last century it has been iterated that 'legal justice between wrongdoer and victim is only a partial and incomplete form of justice'.[154] The notion of social justice has received attention everywhere in the present century. In relation to this growing interest in the idea of justice, traditional "criminal justice theory" arises from the hypothesis that it is the whole society which is harmed by the wrongdoing of criminals.[155] The criminal justice system is often concerned with proving an accused person's guilt and awarding punishment through a process comprising a contest between the State and accused person(s).[156] Along with such punishment, imposing reparation on the guilty to provide it to the victims has gradually been considered as one of the forms of ensuring social justice throughout the criminal justice scheme in the current century.[157] Friedrich Hayek stipulates that the term "social justice"

---

[152] Id; See also, Hugo Adam Bedau, 'Retribution and the Theory of Punishment' (1978) The Journal of Philosophy 75, 616.

[153] Ibid, 77; Maduabuchi Dukor, 'Conceptions of Justice' [2004], available at <http://www.unipu/q/english/IPQ/21-25/PDF/24-4-4.pdf> accessed on 3 May 2017.

[154] Brian Barry, Theories of Justice (Berkeley: University of California Press, 1989) 111.

[155] Ibid, 91; David Schmidtz, Elements of Justice (New York: Columbia University Press, 2006) 45.

[156] George Mousourakis, 'Understanding and Implementing Restorative Justice' [2003-04] 11 Tilburg Foreign Law Review 626, 626.

[157] Id; John Rawls, 'Justice as Fairness: Political not Metaphysical' [1985] 14 (3) Philosophy and Public Affairs 223, 251.

refers to the distribution of economic rewards either by the guilty person as a form of legal justice, or by the government in other situations.[158]

7.4.4 In connection to wartime crimes, during the establishment of the ICTY, the United Nations Security Council stated in its Resolutions 808 and 827 that even prior to the conclusion of conflicts, the Tribunal should commence trials to bring perpetrators to justice.[159] It observed that the tension between peace and justice in the wartime situation in the former Yugoslavia made it clear to the whole world that the 'international justice cannot ignore the surrounding political environment.'[160] Antonio Cassese, the then President of the ICTY, said that 'only justice can break the cycle of revenge and violence.'[161] He added that '[t] he quest for justice for yesterday's victims of atrocities should not be pursued in such a manner that it makes today's living the dead of tomorrow.'[162]

7.5 Conceptualizing 'Complete Justice'

7.5.1 Very recently, it has been observed in the case of the *Jean-Pierre Bemba Gombo*[163] that 'legal justice' is really important for survivors of rape and other sexual violence.[164] Noticeably the

---

[158] Samuel Taylor Morison, 'A Hayekian Theory of Social Justice' [2005] 1 *NYU Journal of Law & Liberty* 225, 226.

[159] Pierre Hazan, 'The Revolution by the ICTY: The Concept of justice in Wartime' [2004] 2 *Journal of International Criminal Justice* 533, 536.

[160] Ibid.

[161] *Id*, 537.

[162] *Id*, 537 – 8; *See also*, Harry Brighouse, *Justice* (Cambridge: Polity Press, 2004) 196.

[163] *The Prosecutor v. Jean-Pierre Bemba Gombo*, ICC-01/05-01/08 (Trial Chamber III), 21 March 2016.

[164] Janine Natalya Clark, 'The Bemba Judgement and 'Justice'

judgment in this case provides recognition of survivors' grief as well as acknowledges their victimhood. Nevertheless, the International Criminal Court (ICC) emphasizes that 'legal justice is only one part of a complex justice mosaic.'[165] The judges noted that '[w]hen their rapes were known within their communities, victims were ostracised, socially rejected, and stigmatised'.[166] Thus, the Trial Chamber of the ICC admitted the margins of legal justice because whether a legal judgement alone can alter 'social attitudes' towards rape survivors is still a question.

7.5.2 These propositions of the ICC draws the concept of 'complete justice' which may remind us of the Latin maxim '*[f]iat justitia ruat cælum*' that means '[l]et justice be done, though the heavens fall.'[167] But there is no set standard of conceptualizing 'complete justice' from a broader perspective. Understanding of justice differs from person to person, place to place, and time to time. As a matter of fact, the notion of justice differs in every culture since the cultures of different places depend upon a collective history, mythology and religion.[168] Besides, the concept of justice is influenced by the moral and ethical values of every culture.

for Survivors of Rape and Sexual Violence' (15 July 2016), available at <http://www.svri.org/blog/bemba-judgement-and-%E2%80%98justice%E2%80%99-survivors-rape-and-sexual-violence> accessed on 28 April 2017.

[165]   Ibid.

[166]   *Jean-Pierre Bemba Gombo* (n 163) para 331, page 149.

[167]   'Supreme Court for 'Complete Justice'' *The Telegraph (India)*, (20 April, 2017), available at <https://www.telegraphindia.com/1170420/jsp/nation/story_147334.jsp> accessed on 21 April 2017.

[168]   Judith Resnik and Dennis Edward Curtis, *Representing Justice: Invention, Controversy, and Rights in City-states* (United States: Yale University Press, 2011) 310.

7.5.3 In this respect, it should be mentioned that in both the *Sesay, Kallon and Gbao (RUF Trial)*[169] and the *Brima, Kamara and Kanu (AFRC trial)*[170] cases, the issue of "forced marriage" of the women and girls in Sierra Leone to the Revolutionary United Front (RUF) and Armed Forces Revolutionary Council (AFRC) fighters was raised in the SCSL.[171] Here lies a question as to whether the events of 'forced marriage' of such women and girls can be considered at all as "justice" to the victims. Nonetheless, the *Taylor*[172] trial judgment proposed that the term 'conjugal slavery' can be used instead of 'forced marriage' since those women and girls had been enslaved for the dual purposes of ongoing rape and forced domestic and other labor.[173] Thus, the very thought of ensuring justice to rape victims of Sierra Leone by making them agree to forcible marriage to soldiers, was a fallacy.

7.5.4 To ensure justice to war rape victims of the Liberation War of Bangladesh, the ICT-BD observed in the case concerning *Qaiser*[174] that:

> '[t]he war time rape victims are our great mothers
> and sisters. We cannot shut our eyes any more.
> The nation, the society must come forward to
> recognise and salute their sacrifices, to heal
> their wound, to compensate the barbaric wrongs
> done to them. The victims of sexual violence

---

[169] *The Prosecutor v. Sesay, Kallon & Gbao*, SCSL-04-15-T (Trial Chamber I), 2 March, 2009.

[170] *The Prosecutor v. Brima, Kamara & Kanu*, SCSL-04-16-T (Trial Chamber II), 20 June, 2007.

[171] Valerie Oosterveld, 'Gender and the Charles Taylor Case at the Special Court for Sierra Leone' [2012] 19(1) *William & Mary Journal of Women and the Law*, 7, 9.

[172] *The Prosecutor v. Taylor*, SCSL-03-01-T (Trial Chamber II), 18 May, 2012, para. 2035.

[173] Ibid, paras. 428 – 30.

[174] *Syed Md. Qaiser* (n 11).

including the victims before us need redress in the form of social-service packages with a view of contributing to their rehabilitation and psychosocial permanence. Many of rape victims have already died. They deserve posthumous honour that may reduce the pains and trauma of their dear and near ones.'[175]

From this observation of the ICT-BD, the inference of 'complete justice' can be presumed, which requires a presence of both 'legal justice' and 'social justice'. In order to expand the concept of 'complete justice' in relation to the victims of war rape, the following observations were given in the *A. T. M. Azharul Islam*[176] case:

> '[c]onsidering the sacrifices of the 'Beerangona' ..., the government should take necessary measures to include in the curriculum of both school and college level about their sacrifices and painful experiences in 1971 during the Liberation War so that the generation to generation can know the real history of the Liberation War of 1971, the sacrifices of 'Beerangona' and the barbaric atrocities including sexual violence committed by the Pakistani occupation army and their local collaborators like the Rajakars, Al-Badrs, Al-Shams and the members of the Peace Committee.'[177]

7.5.5 In short, the concept of 'justice' is relative, and depends on cultures of different places, considering history, mythology and religion, whereas 'complete justice' embraces both 'legal

---

[175] Ibid, para. 987.
[176] *A. T. M. Azharul Islam Case* (n 12).
[177] Ibid, para. 332.

justice' and 'social justice'. On the one hand, as an endeavour to ensure 'legal justice' to the war rape victims of the Liberation War of Bangladesh, some of the perpetrators have already been punished through exemplary trials held in domestic tribunals. On the other hand, even though there is no set definition of 'complete justice', the observations of the ICC in the *Bemba case*, the SCSL in the *Taylor case*, and the ICT-BD in the *Qaiser case* as well as the *A. T. M. Azharul Islam case* imply that when 'social justice' is ensured along with 'legal justice', war rape victims would get proper justice. In other words, awarding both 'legal punishments' to perpetrators and giving 'social recognition as well as respect' to war rape victims altogether may ensure 'complete justice' for them.

8

The ICT-BD Trials On Rape Of The Women

8.1 During the Liberation War of Bangladesh in 1971, perpetrators of sexual violence committed international crimes of an unspeakable magnitude. Most of them, however, was unpunished for a long period. In order to bring, *inter alia*, active members and/or leaders of local auxiliary *para-militia* forces and local collaborators (*inter alia*), however, the International Crimes Tribunal-1 (ICT-1) and subsequently, International Crimes Tribunal-2 (ICT-2) were formed in 2010 and 2012 respectively.[178] Such trials attracted both national and international attention and set a standard of justice for victims of sexual violence, their family members, and people as a whole. It should be mentioned that though the *International Crimes (Tribunals) Act*, 1973 (*ICTA*) came into force on 20 July, 1973, no Tribunal had been set up and no trial took place under the *Act* until the domestic judicial forums were established.

---

[178] Website of the ICT-1, available at <http://ict-bd.org/ict1/> accessed on 20 March 2017; the *International Crimes (Tribunals) Act* (ICTA), Section 6.

8.2 An Indication of the Rape Prosecutions in the ICT-BD

8.2.1 The ICT-1 and ICT-2 decided 24 and 11 cases respectively on the charges brought as "crimes against humanity" and the "crime of genocide".[179] In the process, the ICT-BD decided a total 35 cases till date. However, this research focuses on the 30 cases decided till 10 January 2018. Out of these 30 cases, the Prosecution brought rape charges successfully in 12 cases; which means that 40% cases of the ICT-BD were related to rape prosecutions.

---

[179] Websites of the ICT-1 and ICT-2, available at <http://ict-bd.org/ict1/> and <http://ict-bd.org/ict2/> accessed on 12 March 2017; The ICT-BD is yet to deal with a single charge on the "war crimes".

8.2.2 As per the following table, 8 charges against *Abul Kalam Azad;*[180] 6 against *Abdul Quader Molla;*[181] 20 against *Delowar*

---

[180] *Moulana Abdul Kalam Azad* (n 15), on pages 5-6, paragraph 12: 'Moulana Abul Kalam Azad @ Bachchu was born on 5th March, 1947 at village 'Barakhardia'. He studied in Faridpur Rajendra College and was a close associate of Ali Ahsan Mohammad Mujahid, the then President of East Pakistan Islami Chatra Sangha (ICS). Till formal formation of Razaker force, Moulana Abul Kalam Azad @ Bachchu actively aided the Pakistani army as an armed member of volunteer Razakar Force formed in Faridpur in committing criminal acts alleged. He, during the war of liberation in 1971, assisted the Pakistani occupation force initially in the capacity of 'Razaker' and subsequently as chief of Al-Badar bahini of Faridpur. At one time, Moulana Abul Kalam Azad @ Bachchu was 'rokan' of jamat-E-Islami and now he is not associated with any political party. He is the chairman of 'Masjid Council, a non-government organization [NGO]. On 21 April, 1971 he being united with the local anti-liberation circle welcomed the Pakistani army in Faridpur district. He was a close associate of Pakistani army, and actively and substantially assisted them as a potential member of Razakar (Volunteer) force in committing atrocities targeting the civilians and Hindu community and pro-liberation Bangalee people. In Faridpur, he was in charge of Razaker bahini which was equipped with rifles.'

[181] *Abdul Quader Molla* (n 14), on page 8, paragraph 17: 'Abdul Quader Molla was born in 1948. While he was a student of BSC (Bachelor of Science) in Rajendra College, Faridpur in 1966, he joined the student wing of JEI known as 'Islami Chatra Sangha' (ICS) and he held the position of president of the organization. While he was student of the Dhaka University, he became the president of Islami Chatra Sangha of Shahidullah Hall unit. In 1971, according to the prosecution, he organized the formation of Al-Badar Bahini with the students belonging to Islami Chatra Sangha (ICS) which allegedly being in close alliance with the Pakistani occupation army and Jamat-e-Islami actively aided, abetted, facilitated and substantially assisted, contributed and provided moral support and encouragement in committing appalling atrocities in 1971 in the territory of Bangladesh.'

Hossain Sayeedi;[182] 16 against *Motiur Rahman Nizami;*[183] 11 against

---

[182] *Delowar Hossain Sayeedi* (n 13), on pages 7-8, paragraph 15: 'Delowar Hossain Sayeedi alias Delu @ Abu Nayeem Mohammad Delowar Hossain@ Allama Delowar Hossain Sayeedi was born on 1 February, 1940. He passed Dhakil Examination from Darns Sunnat Madrasha Sarsina in 1957 and he also passed the Alim Examination in 1960 from Barroipara Madrasha. He was elected Member of the parliament in the election held in 1996 and 2001. He joined Jamaat-e-Islam and the Nayb-e-Amir of Jamaat-e- Islami Central Committee. He is a writer by profession and known all over the Muslim world as a renowned Oazin and Orator. On perusal of the papers submitted by the accused with the form filled up in the 9thParliament Election of 2008, it is found that a part of his name "Abu Nayeem Mohammad" is cut off from his name and new names such as 'Allamma' and Sayeedi have been added with his name. In the same form he wrote his name "Allama Delowar Hossain Sayeedi" and signed it. It is alleged by the prosecution that after passing Alim Examination he did not receive any higher degree nor he obtained doctorate degree in any subject of Islam religion and as such he is not legally entitled to use the title 'Allama' or 'Maulana' with his name. During the War of Liberation in 1971 the accused was a grocery shopkeeper, he used to sell oil, salt, onion and pepper at Parerhat Bazar and as such his economic condition was not good. He could speak Urdu well as, he obtained 'Alim' from Madrasha. He welcomed the Pakistani Army at Parerhat Bazar and formed local peace committee and subsequently as a member of Rajakar Bahini actively participated in the atrocities committed by Pakistani Army and Rajaker Bahini targeting civilians, Hindu Community and pro-liberation people. By adopting illegal means became a rich man and now he is the owner of huge properties including multistoried buildings in Dhaka and Khulna.'

[183] *Motiur Rahman Nizami* (n 16), on pages 9-10, paragraph 18: 'Motiur Rahman Nizami was born on 31st March, 1943. In his early life, he studied in Boalmari Madrasha at Sathia and passed his Dakhil examination in 1955, and then he passed Alim examination in 1959 and Fazil examination in 1961. He got his Kamil degree in Figh from Madrasha-e-Alim, Dhaka in 1963. He also obtained graduation degree in 1967 from the University of Dhaka, as a private student.

Zahid Hossain Khokon;[184] 16 against *Syed Md. Qaiser;*[185] 6 against *A.*

During the War of Liberation in 1971, he was the President of Pakistan Islami Chhatra Sangha (ICS), the student wing of Jamaat-e-Islami (JEI) and also the chief of Al-Badr Bahini. The Al-Badr Bahini was mainly formed by the members of Islami Chhatra Sangha under the leadership of the accused. Both Jamaat-e-Islami and Islami Chhatra Sangha actively opposed the Liberation War of Bangladesh and those organizations formed Razakar Bahini, Al-Badr Bahini and Al-Shams. After completion of student life he joined the Jamaat-e- Islami and became Ameer of Dhaka city Unit as well as member of central executive committee of Jamaat-e-Islami from 1978 to 1982. He held the post of Assistant Secretary General of Jamaat-e-Islami from 1983 to 1988. He became the Secretary General of the said party in December, 1988 and held the said post up to 2000. He became the 'Ameer' (Chief) of Jamaat-e-Islami in 2000 and since then he has been holding the post of 'Ameer' of the said party till now. During the War of Liberation, he assisted the then 'Ameer' of Jamaat-e-Islami Professor Ghulam Azam in forming Shanti Committees, Razakars, Al-Badr and Al-Shams to collaborate Pakistan occupation forces. He was elected as a Member of Parliament in 1991 and was the leader of Parliamentary party of Jamaat-e-Islami. He was also elected as a Member of Parliament in 2001 and he became the Minister for Agriculture from 2001- 2003 and Minister for Industries from 2003- 2006 under the Bangladesh Nationalist Party (BNP) led government.'

[184] *Zahid Hossain Khokon* (n 17), on page 4, paragraph 7: 'Zahid Hossain Khokon @ M.A Zahid Khokon @ Khokon Matubbar @ Khokon was born on 11th January, 1942. He was the local leader of Jamaat-e-Islami. He took training of arms for becoming a Razakar in April, 1971. In the month of May, 1971, the accused along with his elder brother late Zafor formed a Razakar Bahini in their locality. After the death of his elder brother RazakarZafor in a combat with freedom fighters, he took absolute leadership of local Razakar Bahini as a commander. He was directly involved in the commission of 'Crimes against Humanity' and genocide as committed in different places of Nagarkanda, Faridpur. Subsequently, he joined Bangladesh Nationalist Party (BNP) giving up Jamaat-e-Islami politics.'

[185] *Syed Md. Qaiser* (n 11), on page 9, paragraph 24: 'Syed Md. Qaiser @ Md. Qaiser @ Syed Qaiser @ SM Qaiser @ Qaiser was born on

19 June 1940. He obtained matriculation from Armanitola New Government High School, Dhaka and studied in Jagannath College Dhaka. He, however, studied up to BA class as found from the registration form filled up and submitted to the Habiganj Election Office. Accused Qaiser is an industrialist and owns a number of industrial concerns. It is alleged that Syed Md. Qaiser became associated with the politics of Convention Muslim League in 1962 and was elected Member of Sylhet District Board in 1966 and occupied the chair till 1971. Qaiser contested Provincial Assembly Election in 1970 as an independent contestant and was defeated. During the war of liberation in 1971 he was allegedly associated with the local occupation army and carried out atrocious criminal activities throughout the period of war in the localities of Habiganj and Brahamanbaria sub-division [now district], as alleged by the prosecution. Instantly either before or after the victory achieved on 16 December 1971, accused Qaiser allegedly went into hiding and fled to London, UK, quitting Bangladesh. The prosecution also alleges that the accused Syed Md. Qaiser returned back home in 1978. In 1979 he contested second parliamentary election as an independent candidate and was elected in Sylhet-17 constituency and afterwards joined the Bangladesh Nationalist Party [BNP] and became the president of Habiganj district BNP. In 1982 he became the joint secretary general of BNP [Shah Azizur Rahman group]. Afterwards, he joined the Jatio Party of General Ershad and was elected as president of Habiganj Jatio Party. In 1986, and 1988 he was elected Member of Parliament contesting the Jatio Parishad election as a candidate of Jatio Party, in Habiganj-4 constituency [Madhabpur-Chunarughat]. Later on, he became the State Minister for the Agricultural Ministry. In 1991, 1996 and 2001 he contested the parliamentary elections as a candidate of Jatio Party, but was defeated. At a stage, he, quitting jatio Party, joined PDP.'

T. M. Azharul Islam;[186] 5 against *Md. Forkan Mallik;*[187] 4 in the case

---

[186] *A. T. M. Azharul Islam Case* (n 12), on page 16, paragraph 27: 'A.T.M Azharul Islam was born on 28th February, 1952. He was a student of H.S.C in Rangpur Carmichael College during 1969 to 1971. At that time, he was the president of Islami Chhatra Sangha (ICS), the student wing of Jamaat-e-Islami (JEI) Rangpur unit and also commander of Al-Badr Bahini of Rangpur district. In 1971, during the War of Liberation of Bangladesh, the accused collaborated Pakistani army to execute their plan and design in committing crimes against Humanity and genocide all over Rangpur district. He, being the commander of Al-Badr Bahini, resisted the War of Liberation and committed atrocities in all over the district through his members of *Al- Badr Bahini.*'

[187] *Forkan Mallik* (n 18), on pages 2-3, paragraph 5: 'Md. Forkan Mollik @ Forkan studied up to class IV. As per prosecution, the accused is an employee in a Non-Government Organization (NGO) in Dhaka and also a farmer, by profession. In 1971, he joined the local Razakar force and used to carry out criminal acts under the local Razakar commanders. He was an active supporter of Muslim League and subsequently since 1977 he has been with the political party BNP.'

concerning *Boro Mia*,[188] *Mujibur Rahman*,[189] and *Md. Abdur Razzak*;[190]

---

[188] *Boro Mia and Others* (n 19), on pages 20-21, paragraph 27: 'Mohibur Rahman alias Boro Mia [65] son of late Daras Uddin and Khodeja Khatun of Village Kumurshana, Police Station Baniachang, District Habiganj was born on 01 January 1950 at that village Kumurshana. He studied up to class X in Baniachang Sandalpur BC High School. He was a strong follower of Syed Kamrul Ahsan, a local potential leader of Nejam-e-Islami, a pro-Pakistani political organisation and he and his brothers sided against the war of liberation and joined the local Razakar Bahini, prosecution alleges. His elder brother Kalamdhar was allegedly the Chairman, Peace Committee of Khagaura Union and younger brother Mostofa [now dead] was the commander of Khagaura Razakar camp.'

[189] *Boro Mia and Others* (n 19), on page 21, paragraph 28: 'Mujibur Rahman alias Angur Mia [60] son of late Daras Uddin and Khodeja Khatun of Village Kumurshana, Police Station Baniachang, District Habiganj was born on 10 March 1955 at said village Kumurshana. He is the younger brother of accused Mohibur Rahman alias Boro Mia. He studied up to class V in Dhulia Ghatua Primary School at Khagaura under Baniachang Police Station of the then Habiganj Sub-Division. He was a committed follower of Syed Kamrul Ahsan, a local potential leader of Nejam-e-Islami, a pro-Pakistani political organisation and he and his brothers took deliberate stance against the war of liberation and joined the local Razakar Bahini, prosecution alleges. According to the prosecution, his elder brother Kalamdhar was the Chairman, Peace Committee of Khagaura Union and his brother Mostofa [now dead] was the commander of Khagaura Razakar camp. After liberation, he started working as a supporter of Jamaat-e- Islami.'

[190] *Boro Mia and Others* (n 19), on page 22, paragraph 29: 'Md. Abdur Razzak [63] son of late Toij Ullah alias Toij Ali and Khodeja Begum of Village Hossainpur, Khagaura, Police Station Baniachang, District Habiganj was born on 13 August 1952 at the said village. He did not achieve any education. He is the cousin brother of accused Mohibur Rahman and Mujibur Rahman. He also joined the local Razakar Bahini along with accused Mohibur Rahman, a potential follower of local leader of Nejam-e-Islami, a pro-Pakistani political organisation, prosecution alleges.'

5 in the case of *Md. Sakhawat Hossain,*[191] *Md. Billal Hossain,*[192] *Md. Lutfor Morol,*[193] *Md. Ibrahim Hossain,*[194] *Sheikh Mohammad Mujibur*

---

[191] *Md. Sakhawat Hossain and Others* (n 20), on pages 476-477, paragraph 797(i): 'Md. Sakhawat Hossain [61], son of late Omar Ali and late Anowara Begum of village Hijoldanga, Police StationKeshobpur, District-Jessore was born on 01.03.1954. He passed Alim Examination in 1967 and Fazil Examination in 1969. He got his Kamil degree from Alia Madrasha, Khulna in 1971, but that examination was cancelled. Thereafter, he obtained his Kamil degree in 1972. He also obtained M.A. degree in 1976 from the department of Islamic Studies of the University of Dhaka. In 1966, he joined Islami Chhatra Sangha [ICS], the student wing of Jamaate-Islami [JEI], the prosecution alleged. After the independence of Bangladesh, he joined the Motijheel Ideal School as an Assistant Teacher. Subsequently, he resigned from that school and joined in the office of Accountant General [A.G] in 1981. He became the 'Rukan' of Jamaat-e-Islami in 1986, the prosecution alleged. He was elected as a Member of Parliament in 1991. Thereafter, he joined the Bangladesh Nationalist Party [BNP]. He was also elected as a Member of Parliament in 1996. In 2008, he joined the Jatio Party [JP] and since then, he has been holding the post as ' Presidium Member' of the JP.'

[192] *Md. Sakhawat Hossain and Others* (n 20), on page 477, paragraph 797 (ii): 'Md. Billal Hossain Biswas [75], son of late Yakub Ali Biswas alias Akabbar alias Akbor and late Rupban Bibi of village Nehalpur, Police Station-Keshobpur, District-Jessore was born on 10.05.1940. He joined the Razakar Bahini during the war of liberation in 1971, the prosecution alleged.'

[193] *Md. Sakhawat Hossain and Others* (n 20), on page 478, paragraph 797(iii): 'Md. Lutfor Morol [69] (now dead), son of late Joynal Morol and late Mokarjan of village Porchokra, Police Station Keshobpur, District-Jessore was a Member of local Razakar Bahini and an accomplice of accused Md.Sakhawat Hossain, at the time of War of Liberation in 1971, the prosecution alleged.'

[194] *Md. Sakhawat Hossain and Others* (n 20), on page 478, paragraph 797(iv): 'Md. Ibrahim Hossain alias Ghungur Ibrahim [60] [absconded], son of lateYakub Ali Biswas alias Akabbar alias Akbor and late Rupban Bibi of village Nehalpur, at present Boga, Police

Rahman,[195] *Md. A. Aziz Sardar,*[196] *Abdul Aziz Sardar,*[197] *Kazi Ohidul Islam,*[198] *and Md. Abdul Khaleque Morol;*[199] 4 in the case concerning

---

Station-Keshobpur, District-Jessore was a member of local Razakar Bahini and an accomplice of accused Md. Sakhawat Hossain at the time of War of Liberation in 1971, the prosecution alleged.'

[195] *Md. Sakhawat Hossain and Others* (n 20), on page 478, paragraph 797(v): 'Sheikh Mohammad Mujibur Rahman alias Mujibur Rahman[absconded][61], son of Sheikh Mohammad Afazulla alias Effaztulla and late Pachibibi of village Sheikhpara, Police Station Keshobpur, District-Jessore was a member of local Razakar Bahini and an accomplice of accused Md. Sakhawat Hossain at the time of War of Liberation in 1971, the prosecution alleged.'

[196] *Md. Sakhawat Hossain and Others* (n 20), on page 478, paragraph 797(vi): 'Md. A. Aziz Sardar [absconded] [65], son of late Ful Miah Sardar and late Nurjahan Begum of village Mominpur, Police Station- Keshobpur, District-Jessore was a member of local Razakar Bahini and an accomplice of accused Md. Sakhawat Hossain at the time of War of Liberation in 1971, the prosecution alleged.'

[197] *Md. Sakhawat Hossain and Others* (n 20), on pages 478-479, paragraph 797(vii): 'Abdul Aziz Sardar [absconded] [66], son of late Ahmmad Sardar and late Sakina of village Boga, Police Station-Keshobpur, District-Jessore was a member of local Razakar Bahini and an accomplice of accused Md. Sakhawat Hossain at the time of War of Liberation in 1971, the prosecution alleged.'

[198] *Md. Sakhawat Hossain and Others* (n 20), on page 479, paragraph 797(viii): 'Kazi Ohidul Islam alias Kazi Ohidus Salam [absconded] [61], son of late Kazi Motiassalam alias Motiar Salam and late Hosneara Begum of village Sheikhpara, Police StationKeshobpur, District-Jessore was a member of local Razakar Bahini and an accomplice of accused Md. Sakhawat Hossain at the time of War of Liberation in 1971, the prosecution alleged.'

[199] *Md. Sakhawat Hossain and Others* (n 20), on page 479, paragraph 797(ix): 'Md. Abdul Khaleque Morol [absconded] [68], son of late Hachan Ali Morol and late Rebeya Begum of village Altapoul, Police Station-Keshobpur, District-Jessore was a member of local Razakar Bahini and an accomplice of accused Md. Sakhawat Hossain at the time of War of Liberation in 1971, the prosecution alleged.'

Md. Solaiman Mollah[200] and *Md. Idris Ali Sardar and others;*[201] and 6

---

[200] *Md. Idris Ali Sardar and Other* (n 21), on page 296, paragraph 613(1): 'Md. Solaiman Mollah(now dead)[now dead] Accused Md. Solaiman Mollah(now dead)(84), son of late Chand Mollah and late Shaharjan Bibi of Kashipur Muslim Para, Ward No. 5, Police Station-Palong, District- Shariatpur was born on 12.06.1931. He passed Dawra Examination. Since 1963 he joined Muslim League [Fazlul Quader group] and became Organizing Secretary of Palong Thana Muslim League, the prosecution alleges. In the year 1970 he joined Jomiatul Ulama-e-Islami and contested in the election to be a member of the Provincial Assembly, but he was defeated. He formed local Peace Committee and Razakar Bahini and led them in aiding Pakistani occupation army in his locality i.e. Palong Thana area of the then Madaripur Sub-Division, the prosecution alleged.'

[201] *Md. Idris Ali Sardar and Others* (n 21), on pages 296-297, paragraph 613(2): 'Idris Ali Sardar [67], son of late Haji Hakim Ali Sardar and late Maju Bibi of village West Kashabhog, Police Station Palong, District- Shariatpur was born on 01.04. 1948 [as per S.S.C. certificate] and on 03.03.957[as per NID]. He passed S.S.C. Examination in 1966. He was an activist of Islami Chhatra Sangha [ICS] while he was a student of Rudrakar Nilmoni High School, Shariatpur in the year 1962-1966, the prosecution alleged. In the year 1969, he was a leader of Islami Chhatra Sangha. During War of Liberation in 1971, he was an active leader of Islami Chhatra Sangha. He joined local Razakar Bahini to collaborate with the Pakistani occupation army, the prosecution alleged. Since the War of Liberation of Bangladesh, he was a leader of Jamaat-e- Islami [JEI].'

in the case of *Md. Moslem Prodhan*[202] *and Syed Md. Hussain*[203] were brought by the ICT-BD Prosecution team. Thus, the total number of charges was 107 in the 12 cases.

8.2.3 It can be seen from the table that the Prosecution brought only 1 rape charge against *Abul Kalam Azad*, 1 rape charge

---

[202] *Md. Moslem Prodhan and another* (n 111), on page 11, paragraph 15(1): 'Md. Moslem Prodhan (67) son of late Labhu Sheikh and late Rezia Akhter of village Kamarhati, Police Station-Nikli, and District-Kishoreganj was born on 31.12.1948. He did not receive any formal education. He is only an alphabet-literate. During the War of Liberation in 1971, accused Md. Moslem Prodhan individually and jointly committed crimes of genocide and crimes against humanity in different localities of the then Kishoreganj SubDivision, and then he was known as 'Razakar Commander' of 'Nikli Union', the prosecution alleges. He has been involved in the politics of Bangladesh Nationalist Party [BNP]'

[203] *Md. Moslem Prodhan and another* (n 111), on pages 11-12, paragraph 15(2): 'Syed Md. Hussain alias Hossain [64] son of late Syed Musleh Uddin and late Syeda Fatema Banu was born on 15.09.1951. His permanent address is village Machihata, Police Station and District Brahmanbaria. His last known current address is House No. 2, Road No. 6, Pink City, Police Station Khilkhet, Dhaka. However, during 1971, he lived at Hoybat Nagar, Police Station Kishoreganj Sadar under the then Kishoreganj Sub-Division of District Mymensingh, prosecution alleges. He passed S.S.C Examination in 1967 from Kishoreganj High School and H.S.C Examination in 1969 from the Gurudoyal College, Kishoreganj. Later, he also passed B.A Examination in 1975 from the same college. During pre-liberation period he was involved with Chhatra League [student wing of Awami League] politics of his college, however, during the Liberation War of 1971, he adopted the ideological position of Pakistan Democratic Party [PDP] and he individually and jointly committed a number of crimes of genocide and crimes against humanity in different localities of the then Kishoreganj Sub-Division, and then he was commonly known as 'Razakar Daroga' of Nikli Thana, prosecution alleges ...'

against *Abdul Quader Molla*, 4 rape charges against *Delowar Hossain Sayeedi*, 2 rape charges against *Motiur Rahman Nizami*, 1 rape charge against *Zahid Hossain Khokon*, 2 rape charges against *Syed Md. Qaiser*; 1 rape charge against *A. T. M. Azharul Islam*; 2 rape charges against *Md. Forkan Mallik*; 1 rape charge in the case of the *Mohibur Rahman alias Boro Mia, Mujibur Rahman alias Angur Mia and Md. Abdur Razzak and others*; 1 rape charge in the case of the *Md. Sakhawat Hossain, Md. Billal Hossain Biswas, Md. Lutfor, Md. Ibrahim Hossain, Sheikh Mohammad Mujibur Rahman, Md. A. Aziz Sardar, Abdul Aziz Sardar, Kazi Ohidul Islam, and Md. Abdul Khaleque Morol*, 1 rape charge in the case of the *Md. Idris Ali Sardar and Md. Solaiman Mollah*, and finally 1 rape charge in the case of the *Md. Moslem Prodhan and Syed Md. Hussain.* Therefore, out of 107 charges, a total of 18 rape charges were brought against the accused. Hence, it is clear that 16.82% rape charges were brought against the said convicts.

8.2.4 From the table, it is clear that out of 18 rape charges, the Prosecution successfully proved 15 charges during the ICT-BD trial by producing adequate number of witnesses and adducing proper evidences as well as submitting their respective arguments. Thus, the conviction rate of the ICT-BD rape prosecutions is remarkably, 83.33%.

TABLE

SL	Case Name	Total Number of Charges	Total Number of Rape Charges	Total Number of Rape Conviction Charges
1	*Delowar Hossain Sayeedi*	20	4	2
2	*Abdul Quader Molla*	6	1	1
3	*Moulana Abdul Kalam Azad*	8	1	1

4	A. T. M. Azharul Islam	6	1	1
5	Motiur Rahman Nizami	16	2	1
6	Syed Md. Qaiser	16	2	2
7	Zahid Hossain Khokon	11	1	1
8	Md. Forkan Mallik	5	2	2
9	Boro Mia and Others	4	1	1
10	Md. Sakhawat Hossain and Others	5	1	1
11	Md. Idris Ali Sardar and Other	4	1	1
12	Md. Moslem Prodhan and Other	6	1	1
TOTAL		107	18	15

8.3 Remarkable Observations of the ICT-BD Regarding Rape Charges

8.3.1 The landmark case of the ICT-BD on 1971 war rapes is the case concerning *Syed Md. Qaiser.* It was found in this case that a Pakistani soldier had said, "*[h]um ja rahe hain lekin beej chhor kar ja rahe hain*" ("[w]e are leaving but leaving our seeds") during the surrender of the West Pakistani troops to the Indian army.[204] During this war, Pakistani soldiers raped aged widows, married women, and schoolgirls with the help of their local collaborators.[205] Pakistani soldiers forcefully confined the women for months within regimental barracks, bunks and even tanks in order to sexually abuse them.[206] The ICT-BD pointed out that the perpetrators used rape as a "weapon" of attacking the people

---

[204] *Syed Md. Qaiser* (n 11), paragraph 682; *See also*, Md. Pizuar Hossain, 'Rape as "War Weapon" and "Genocidal Tool" Covered as War Tactics: The Bangladesh Experience', (2017) 3(1) *Bangladesh Journal of Dalit and Minority* 7, 16.

[205] Ibid.

[206] *Id.*

of Bangladesh.[207] In other words, it can be said that rape was used as a "weapon instead of a bullet" as they intended to break-down the societal bond of people by creating social and gender stigmas and defeating the morale of families, communities, and the entire Bengali entity.[208] The observation of the Tribunal on this issue reads as follows:

> 'War time rape victims cannot be viewed as a mere woman who lost her chastity. In fact they fought by laying their highest self-worth, for the cause of our independence. Time has come to unlock our collective voice to recognise and honour our great mothers and sisters, the war heroines. Social ostracism particularly against village women living in economically down trodden condition acts as the main barrier in digging out the forgotten narratives of sexual invasion committed upon them, in 1971 during the war of liberation.'[209]

8.3.2 The case of *Syed Md. Qaiser* is significant for the reason that the aftermath of mass rape on the victim *Majeda Begum*[210] and her daughter *Shamsun Nahar*[211] (war baby) was discovered in this case.[212] *Majeda Begum* was considered as a primary victim who had to give up normal life, and lost the husband's affection,

---

[207] *Syed Md. Qaiser* (n 11), paragraph 709; *See also, Forkan Mallik* (n 18), paragraph 152; *Boro Mia and Others* (n 19), paragraph 382; *Md. Sakhawat Hossain and Others* (n 20), paragraph 191.

[208] *Syed Md. Qaiser* (n 11), paragraphs 709 and 714; *See also, Forkan Mallik* (n 18), paragraph 382; *Md. Sakhawat Hossain and Others* (n 20), paragraph 191.

[209] Ibid, paragraph 720.

[210] Majeda Begum was the Prosecution Witness 5 (P.W. 5).

[211] Shamsun Nahar was the Prosecution Witness 10 (P.W. 10).

[212] *Syed Md. Qaiser* (n 11), paragraphs 714 - 715.

and saw the conjugal bondage with her husband swapped.[213] The Tribunal, thus, specified the following:

> '... we have found that Majeda Begum a brave mother of the soil has shown courage in making narratives of her immense trauma still she is carrying, by overcoming the vulnerability. Not only she, but her daughter the war baby Shamsun Nahar has also testified her post-birth trauma. We consider their valor as a battle against the existing social ostracism. They deserve salute. The society, the nation, the state and the humanity must and must value their tormenting sacrifice, breaking silence.'[214]

8.3.3 The war baby *Shamsun Nahar* was considered as a secondary victim in this case. It has been depicted that birth of a child as a result of rape is a curse and therefore, she is still living with immense grief of separation and loss in our society.[215] The Tribunal also noted that, '[a] social stigma is also placed on the child born as a result of the use of rape as a weapon of war and it amplifies the trauma and impoverishment of her mother too.'[216] The Tribunal mentioned that:

> 'Already more than four decades have been elapsed. But the war rape victims and the war babies who are still alive, we presume, have been suffering from long-term psychological effects of rape that often include many types

---

[213] *Syed Md. Qaiser* (n 11), paragraph 714; Please note that in the *Forkan Mallik Case*, the ICT-BD reiterated the same findings as regards the aftermath of rape upon *Aleya Begum*, paragraph 218.

[214] Ibid, paragraph 721.

[215] *Id*, paragraph 71.

[216] *Id*, paragraph 717.

of disorders, such as, panic attacks, flashbacks, feeling of shame and dishonour, sense of insecurity and many other disorders affecting normal livelihood. These effects can last even lifelong if the victims and war babies born as a result of sexual violence do not get support and care form the society and the state.'[217]

'Hundreds of thousands of rape survivors remained socially ostracized and unattended. The nation must raise a collective voice that they are war heroines. They are brave 'freedom fighters' as they too sacrificed their supreme self-worth, for the cause of our independence. We recall with laudable appreciation that the father of the nation Bangabandhu Sheikh Mujibur Rahman, in recognition of their glorified sacrifices, honoured them as 'war heroines', immediately after the independence. After the War of Liberation, Bangabandhu Sheikh Mujibur Rahman pleaded with his countrymen to give due honor and dignity to the women oppressed by the Pakistani army [Bangladesh Observer, February 28, 1972, p.1]. In 1972, the Bangladesh Government established the Women's Rehabilitation Board to institutionalize women's rehabilitation project, with the Central Women's Rehabilitation Organization coordinating the Government's post-war policies. But After the assassination of Sheikh Mujib [the father of the nation], the rehabilitation programme was effectively closed, the records were seized and

---

[217] *Syed Md. Qaiser* (n 11), paragraph 985.

all the Dhaka and district centres were turned over to the Women's Directorate ...'[218]

8.3.4 The story of *Golapi Rani* was narrated in the *Forkan Mallik* case.[219] *Golapi Rani* is a victim of mass rape who was taken away from her house.[220] Subsequently, she was left abandoned in front of her house in bleeding condition and as a consequence, she died due to torture and the trauma she sustained.[221] Therefore, the ICT-BD concluded that the Pakistani soldiers used rape as an instrument of threat[222] in order to cripple Bangladeshi families.[223]

8.3.5 The ICT-BD observed in the *Boro Mia and Others* case that '[r]ape or sexual violence, either in war or in peace time, is a beastly act of robbery that takes away the thing that cannot be given back.'[224] According to the ICT-BD, the purpose of the Pakistani Army was to send a message of terrorization to the pro-liberation forces and society as a whole through raping Bangladeshi women.[225] The story of *Agarchand Bibi*, a rape victim, who committed suicide a few days after she was raped by the Pakistani Army, was also discovered in this case.[226] The Tribunal noted in the *Md. Sakhawat Hossain and Others* case that *Ashura Khatun* died in 2011 but the trauma and agony she had undergone still traumatize her dear and near ones.[227]

---

[218] Ibid, paragraph 986.

[219] *Forkan Mallik* (n 18), paragraph 153.

[220] Ibid.

[221] *Forkan Mallik* (n 18), paragraph 154.

[222] *Id*, para. 144.

[223] *Id*, para. 158.

[224] *Id*, para. 381.

[225] Ibid.

[226] *Id*, para. 384.

[227] Ashura Khatun's husband was Prosecution Witness No. 10 (P.W. 10) and her son was Prosecution Witness No. 12 (P.W. 12); *Md. Sakhawat Hossain and Others* (n 19), para. 191.

Such outrageous incidents have left permanent wounds on the minds and bodies of victims, traumatized their families, whole communities, and the nation as a whole during the 1971 Liberation War and afterwards.[228]

---

228 *Md. Sakhawat Hossain and Others* (n 20), para. 191.

9

Overall Findings Of The Survey

9.1 It has already been mentioned that for empirical approach, many rape victims of the Liberation War of Bangladesh were interviewed. This research project involved interviewing total 385 rape victims (and their families) of total 53 Districts of all the 8 Divisions of Bangladesh. Thus, it can be said that this research work surveyed rape victims of 82.8% Districts of Bangladesh as a whole.

9.2 The following table shows the number of rape victims interviewed in each Division of Bangladesh:

Serial No.	Division	Number of Respondents
1	Barishal	30
2	Chittagong	61
3	Dhaka	49
4	Khulna	16
5	Mymensingh	22
6	Rajshahi	42
7	Rangpur	123
8	Sylhet	42
TOTAL:		385

9.3 The Division-wise percentage of the total rape victims who were surveyed for this particular research project stands as 7.8% from Barishal, 15.84% from Chittagong, 12.73% from Dhaka, 4.15% from Khulna, 5.71% from Mymensingh, 10.90% from Rajshahi, 31.95% from Rangpur, and 10.90% from Sylhet. Out of the total 385 respondents, 71.43% were Muslims and 28.57% were non-Muslims. However, this research work did not intend to find out any Division or District-wise trend of minimum or maximum ratio of 1971 Liberation War rape victims of Bangladesh. Here it should be mentioned that project researchers also interviewed a number of ICT-BD Prosecutors, investigators, and even judges who had dealt, in their professional capacities, with war rape cases of the 1971 Liberation War.

9.3.1 The following table shows the Division-wise percentage of the total rape victims who were surveyed for this particular research project:

Serial No.	Division	Percentage of the total rape victims surveyed
1	Barishal	07.8%
2	Chittagong	15.84%
3	Dhaka	12.73%
4	Khulna	04.15%
5	Mymensingh	05.71%
6	Rajshahi	10.91%
7	Rangpur	31.95%
8	Sylhet	10.91%
TOTAL:		**100%**

9.4 It must be mentioned that none of the 385 rape victims surveyed wanted to hide their identities. When asked to do so, they all agreed to disclose their names, experiences, details about their families for research purposes. It is indeed quite a courageous stand on their part. The major trends reflected in this empirical study will be discussed in detail in the next section below.

9.5 Background of the Rape Victims Surveyed

9.5.1 Most of the rape victims surveyed in this research project were uneducated and simple village women. Their economic condition was not at all impressive. Most rape victims surveyed in this research did not receive any formal education at all. For example, Momena Khatun of Kushtia district and Shushoma of Patuakhali district studied up to 7th grade; Mst. Morjina Begum of Dinajpur District, Momena Begum of Dhaka district, Shova Rani Karmakar of Patuakhali district and Nazma Khatun of Chapainawabganj district studied up to 8th grade; Meera Rani Barua of Rangamati district studied up to 9th grade; Asma Khatun of Dinajpur district studied up to the Intermediate level; only Ferdousi (Priyobhashini) Begum of Faridpur district had graduated from a university and Rawshan Ara Begum of Dhaka district had completed her Masters.

9.5.2 The rape victims surveyed in this research were married as well as un-married women. Some of them were engaged at the time the war broke out and were getting ready for their wedding ceremony when they were raped. Many (48%) of the married rape victims also had children from previous marriages when they were raped in 1971. Many were (12%) also pregnant at the time of rape but due to physical torture, they would essentially lose their un-born babies.

9.5.3 In most (99.74%) cases this survey found that rape victims belong to the groups which supported the war of liberation. However, in only one of the cases this survey discovered that the rape victim actually belonged to or was connected with the anti-liberation forces of 1971. Rape victim, Meherjaan

Khatun of Bagerhat district, was actually the wife of a *Razakaar*; nevertheless, she was raped by the Pakistan Army in 1971!

9.6 Range of Age of the Rape Victims Surveyed

9.6.1 The survey found that women who were raped during the Liberation War of 1971 belonged to different age groups. Their ages varied and were between 7 and 80. Among the target respondents of this research, the age range stretched from 9 years to 54 years. For example, Sabeda of Baniachong, Habiganj district, Elijaan Nesa of Kushtia district and Asiron Begum of Jamalpur district were only 9 years old, and Jomila Khatun of Barguna district and Zorifon of Panchgarh district were only 11 years old when they were raped in 1971 during the war of liberation. Ayesha Khatun and Roison of Bagerhat district, Shurbala Singh of Mymensingh district, Bidya Shundori Shutrodhor and Shova Rani Shutrodhor of Kishoreganj district, Shahajaadi Begum of Narshingdi district, Bhokti Rani Pal of Tangail district, Khotina Begum of Lalmonirhat district, Chittobala of Thakurgaon district and Asia Begum of Shirajganj district were all 34 years old when they were raped in 1971. Gyanoda Barmoni of Syedpur, Nilphamari district, Rabeya Bewa of Thakurgaon district, Probashi Malakar of Moulbhibazaar district, Rawshan Ara of Gopalganj district, Haulamaso Aung Marma of Mohalchhori, Khagrachhori district, Bahaton Bewa and Komola Begam of Shirajganj district were all 40 years old and Asiran of Sherpur district was 43 years old when they were raped in 1971. This survey came across Modhu Bala Dey of Shariatpur district as the oldest rape victim of 1971 among all the rape victims surveyed. She was 54 years old in 1971.

9.7 Place and Duration of Torture (Rape)

9.7.1 As far as the place of torture is concerned, the survey found that there were commonly two places where women were raped. According to our research finding, there were many women (53%) who were raped in their home (spot rape) although a number of women (47%) were raped in the camp of the perpetrators (continuous rape).

9.7.2 Among the rape victims were many who were taken to camps, raped and detained there from one day to eight months. For example, Safia Khatun of Kumilla district was continuously raped for three months; Bishamuni Bagti and Shuvodra Bunarji of Moulbhibazaar district, Bokul of Faridpur district, Haulamaso Aung Marma of Mohalchhori, Khagrachhori district, Mallika Ganguly of Barguna district, Sreejita Roy of Patuakhali district and Nazma Begum of Pirojpur district were raped continuously for four months; Moumita Rani Bala of Patuakhali district for six months; Pushpo Rani Boiddo of Chunarughat, Habiganj district for six and a half month; Shabitri Nayek of Habiganj, Ferdousi (Priyobhashini) Begum of Faridpur district, Asma Khatun of Dinajpur district and Latifa Begum of Rajshahi district were raped continuously for as long as eight months in various camps.

9.8 Medical Treatment Received by the Rape Victims Surveyed

9.8.1 On 7 January 1972, the "Central Organization for Women's Rehabilitation" (*Kendrio Mohila Punorbashon Songstha*) was established. Sufia Kamal became its chairperson and Taslima Abed, a member of Parliament, became its treasurer.[229] In addition, Shahera Ahmed of the Social Welfare Ministry, was the

---

[229] Syedur Rahman and Craig Baxter, 'Historical Dictionary of Bangladesh,' (2002) *Scarecrow* 1, 52.

secretary; Hajera Khatun was in charge of domestic and medical arrangements for rescued rape victims.[230]

9.8.2 Afterwards, the Government established the "Bangladesh Women's Rehabilitation Board"[231] on 18 February 1972 as a semi-autonomous organization.[232] This organization was associated with the Ministry of Social Welfare.[233] The governing board of the organization was constituted of 13 members headed by Justice K. M. Sobhan, then a sitting Supreme Court judge, while other members included prominent women political leaders and war widows.[234]

9.8.3 It must be mentioned that the rehabilitation centers primarily provided medical aid to war rape victims, including arranging abortion in case of unwanted pregnancies, treatment for diseases, and other socio-economic support. However, in our survey, most (83%) respondents revealed that they were provided with private treatments in their locality.

9.8.4 The reasons for seeking treatment thus were various, mainly due to, non-accessibility of formal or governmental medical facilities during war and social embarrassment. Many (96%) rape victims interviewed mentioned that as they were raped while the War of Liberation was going on, they could not

---

230 Ibid, 53.
231 Please be informed that this Board subsequently became the "Women's Rehabilitation and Welfare Foundation".
232 Rahman and Baxter (n 229), 53.
233 Ibid.
234 The board members were: Justice K. M. Sobhan, Budrunnessa Ahmad, Nurjahan Murshed, Sajeda Chowdhury, Momtaz Begum, Rafia Akhtar Dolly, Nilima Ibrahim, Sufia Kamal, Jahanara Rabbi, Lily Chowdhury, Basanti Guhathakurta, Mushfequa Mahmud and Abdul Awal (Executive Director); 'High Powered Body to Rehabilitate Women Victims,' *The Bangladesh Observer*, 24 February 1972, 1.

actually access any formal or governmental medical facilities. Moreover, commuting during war time was actually a challenge. So, they had to manage with local informal medical support.

9.8.5 Also, many (73%) rape victims mentioned that they did not want to go out and seek formal medical assistance after the war due to pressure from their families to keep rape incidents secret. Their families did not want any kind of social embarrassment and as such, did not allow the rape victim/s within their family to go out and seek proper medical treatment. Therefore, most (96%) rape victims surveyed had to manage with whatever local and secret informal medical support they could manage. This resulted in long-term health complications for many (83%) of the rape victims.

9.9 Family Rehabilitation of the Rape Victims Surveyed

9.9.1 On the question of acceptance of war rape victims by their families, either parental or in-laws, most (79%) war rape victims interviewed were found to have been accepted by their respective families, although there are also some cases where they (21%) were not accepted by their respective families. But even in cases, where the families accepted them, they were not well-treated and their family members were quite unhappy to deal with them.

9.9.2 The survey of this research project found significant variations in the treatment of rape victims in their families by male and female members. In many cases (41%), it was seen that rape victims were well-treated by male members and in some cases (21%), they were neglected by female members of their families. There are also a number of opposite scenarios. However, in most cases (79%) female family members treated war rape victims better than male family members. For example, Sabeda of Habiganj district received very sympathetic treatment from her female family members; even though the male members of her family treated her very cruelly.

9.9.3 The nature of the treatment by new members of the family brings in a different dimension to the scenario. The survey found that apart from old members of families of war rape victims, new members including daughter-in-laws, son-in-laws and their relatives used to mistreat them. Even sons and daughters of war rape victims were insulted by their in-laws and relatives for their mother being raped during the Liberation War of Bangladesh in 1971. In many cases, incidents of rape were not disclosed to new relatives. Nevertheless, the moment the matter got known, the treatment towards rape victims and their families turned out to be quite unsympathetic. The survey found out that only in two cases did daughter-in-laws were found very sympathetic towards rape victims who were their mother-in-laws. Madhubala Dey and Romola Dey of Shariatpur district were such two lucky ones to get respect, love and care from their own daughter-in-laws.

9.10 Society's Reaction towards the Rape Victims Surveyed

9.10.1 The survey found that the society as a whole was and is still very unwilling to treat war rape victims. Almost all respondents (100%) expressed their long-lasting agony of being offended by members of their community. Immediately after the war, some male members of their community made many indecent proposals to them, treating them like prostitutes. Not only the male members, some female members of some community used indecent words addressing them and abused them.

9.10.2 The survey found that social ostracism is one of the toughest situations for war rape victims to tackle. Of course, it was not their fault if they were raped. However, the most of them had to face social ostracism all through their lives. Some war rape victims tried to hide rape incidents and wanted to start life anew, which they have the right to do. However, the moment their past was disclosed, the process of cruel social exclusion began and some left no stone unturned to humiliate them in every way. For example, Nurjahan of Shirajganj district got married after disclosing the incident of her victimization to her husband before her marriage. So, the wedding took place because her husband chose her. However, after a few years of her marriage family members of the husband of Nurjahan discovered the truth and forced her husband to divorce her.

9.10.3 The survey found that not only the rape victims, but children they had out of legal wedlock also suffered social banishment and exclusion for no fault of their own. Aleya, the daughter of war rape victim Monowara of Feni district, got divorced when her in-laws got to know that she was a daughter of a war rape victim. This was also the experience of Moyna, the daughter of war rape victim Mahela Bewa of Shirajganj district and children of the war rape victim Tara Banu of Hobiganj district.

9.10.4 It may be mentioned that three war rape victims who came to Dhaka to testify against the war criminals during the public trial of war criminals in 1992, all were socially ostracized after their return to their hometown. Their sons lost their job and their daughters got divorced. Such was the experience of Dulijan Nesa, Elijan Nesa and Masuda Khatun of Kushtia district.

9.10.5 According to the survey findings, war rape victims are addressed in a derogatory manner by society. They are called names such as, prostitutes, sixers of Paki armies, wives of Paki armies, etc. It is in fact heart-breaking to note that these women who had sacrificed themselves for the liberation of Bangladesh were never received the proper respect from Bangladeshi society. According to some survey respondents though they were named

"*Birangonas*" [War Heroines], this very word actually was used to shame them after the independence of Bangladesh.

9.10.6 It may be mentioned here that on 27 January 2014, the "*Bangladesh National Women Lawyers' Association* (BNWLA)" filed a '*Public Interest Litigation (PIL)*' under Articles 102(1) and 102(2)(a)(i) of the *Constitution of the People's Republic of Bangladesh* of 1972 demanding enacting a law to recognize '*Birangonas*' as 'freedom fighters'.[235] Following this action, the High Court Division (HCD) of the Supreme Court of Bangladesh issued a rule asking the Government of Bangladesh to explain in 4 weeks, starting from 18 May 2014, as to why '*Birangonas*' would be not recognized as 'freedom fighters' and accordingly, provided with all the same facilities, benefits, and privileges as the latter group.[236]

9.10.7 On 29 January 2015, the Government of Bangladesh passed a law in Parliament for the purpose of recognizing '*Birangonas*' as 'freedom fighters'.[237] In order to implement such a law, a total 185 '*Birangonas*' were recognized as 'freedom fighters' till 9 July 2017 by issuing 'Gazette Notifications' in several stages.[238] It should be mentioned that all '*Birangonas*' who received recognition as 'freedom fighters' are entitled to get all the facilities that a freedom fighter usually enjoys in Bangladesh such as monthly allowance, tuition fees waiver for their children, and so on.

---

[235] 'Recognising the Role of Women in the Liberation War,' *Community Legal Services*, available at <http://communitylegalservice.org/hello-world/> accessed on 27 December 2018.

[236] Ibid.

[237] '24 More 'Birangonas' Recognised as Freedom Fighters,' *The Dhaka Tribune* (24 November 2016), <https://www.dhakatribune.com/bangladesh/2016/11/24/24-birangonas-recognised-freedom-fighters/>.

[238] Ibid.

9.11 Financial Sustainability of the Rape Victims Surveyed

9.11.1 Our survey found that maintaining livelihood of the rape victims after the end of the war was a great challenge for them. Many (32%) 1971 war rape victims lost their husbands, who were killed by the perpetrators of war. Thus, the war resulted in not only making them rape victims but also widows. They, therefore, had to earn their livelihood working in households. Some women even used to beg for meals (for example, Shabitri Nayek of Habiganj district). Women whose husbands were alive used to earn their livelihood with the earnings of their husbands. The unmarried women were maintained by their fathers and brothers.

9.11.2 The survey found that the financial support provided to war rape victims, whether by the Government and/or the Private sector, was meager. The survey discovered that there were a very few women (2%) who were provided such monetary support. However, most of the respondents did not get any financial assistance till date.

9.11.3 According to survey findings, in the non-governmental sector, a number of organizations did try to provide some kind of financial assistance to a number of rape victims of 1971. However, the effort was quite meager. For example, in our survey we found only 11 rape victims of 1971 receiving such financial assistance. This amounts to only 2% of our surveyed rape victims. Also, it is interesting to find that most rape victims belong to Kurigram district. For example, Janata Bank provided Tk. 50,000/- each to Mst. Asma Begum, Mst. Asia Begum, Mst. Basiran Begum, Mst. Gendi Bewa, Mst. Khoteja Begum, Mst. Khuki Begum, Mst. Meherjaan, Mst. Moyna Begum, Mst. Shurujun Bewa and Toru Bala Roy, all of Kurigram district. Similarly, as per our survey findings, Bashundha Group of Companies provided Tk. 1,00,000/- to Ms. Mst. Khuki Begum of Kurigram district.

9.12 Marriage and Re-Marriage of the Rape Victims Surveyed

9.12.1 As already mentioned, many rape victims were unmarried (27%) and very young in 1971. The survey found that the question of moving on with their lives after the rape incident was surely a formidable challenge for them. Family and social rejection actually led many 1971 rape victims to opt for suicide. Many (43%) did not get married afterwards, as they were considered to be untouchables or spoiled by society.

9.12.2 The survey found that some (16%) unmarried rape victims did get married afterwards. Nevertheless, these marriages were not very happy ones. In most cases, the families of the rape victims paid a huge amount of money and offered gifts to the grooms to get the rape victims married and yet such marriages did not last for long. It was also found that a number of marriages took place without the woman disclosing the fact of rape. Unfortunately, the moment the husband or his family got to know the truth, they abandoned the woman. For example, Kanchanmala of Munshiganj district, Ramala Devi of Narayanganj district and Nurjahan of Shirajganj district all were divorced when their husband(s) and in-laws came to know about the incident of rape.

9.12.3 An interesting and painful case can be cited in this regard. It is not always that rape victims suppressed the rape incident they underwent after marriage. In one case the husband took the rape victim as his wife after knowing the whole truth; nevertheless, he divorced her after a while for no good reason. Nurjahan of Shirajganj district had to go through this experience.

9.12.4 This survey also found that many (39%) married rape victims had to marry for a second (or third or fourth) time after either being rejected by their former husbands or due to the death of their husbands in the 1971 war. However, these marriages were only compromises worked out to get the rape victims accommodated in society somehow. They became the second or third wives of the men they got married, did not receive any respect, and in most cases they were used only to provide sexual pleasure to their so-called husbands.

9.12.5 Also, it is noticeable that the age difference between the rape victims and their husbands was huge. For example, Nazma Begum of Pirojpur district, Rashida Devi Chakma of Rangamati district, Meera Rani Barua of Rangamati district, Tara Banu of Habiganj district, Asiron of Sherpur district, Asma Khatun and Mst. Moyna Begum of Dinajpur district and Mst. Zahera Begum of Nilphamari district got married to someone who was almost 25 years older to them. Similarly, the husband(s) of Eshnu of Jokeygonj, Sylhet district, Kanchanmala of Munshiganj district, Konarani Das of Narshingdi district, Noorjahan Begum of Barishal district, Amena Begum of Dinajpur district, Mst. Hapon of Syedpur, Nilphamari district, Sabia of Chilahati, Nilphamari district and Debai of Panchgarh district were almost 35 years older to them. The age difference with the husband(s) of Sabeda of Baniachong, Habiganj district, Apela Begum of Panchgarh district, Mst. Marjina Begum of Dinajpur district and Chanmoni Shokhina of Thakurgaon district was almost 45 years. The survey also came across Monowara of Munshibazaar, Moulbhibazaar district, Monowara of Feni district and Shobita Rani Dhar of Jhalokathi district who were all around 55 years younger than their husband(s)!

9.12.6 This research work found that at times rape victims who became widows during the 1971 War of Liberation had to marry their own brother-in-laws for various reasons. For example, rape victims Moymona Bibi of Habiganj district and Rawshan Ara of Tangail district got married to their own brother-in-laws to protect their children from earlier marriages from uncertainty.

9.12.7 Among rape victims married after their rape incident, the worst experience was found in case of Apela Begum of Nilphamari district. Though she was married four times, basically it was a sex slave. She had no social or legal protection against such heinous treatment.

9.13 War Babies

9.13.1 The question of war babies is not a new thing. This research project also tried to explore this issue. Even though it is assumed that most rape victims would not be willing to disclose the identity of the war baby (if any), this research has newly explored the tale of some war babies. While doing this survey we came across as many as 19 rape victims who got pregnant as a result of war rapes during 1971. Out of a total number of rape victim respondents, this is almost 5%.

9.13.2 It was very much expected that rape victims becoming pregnant as a result of rape would prefer abortion and terminate such pregnancies. The government of Bangladesh also made legal provisions to make such a process legally acceptable right after the War of Liberation. In this regard, pregnancies which could not be terminated due to the health condition of the rape victims, the government of Bangladesh enacted new law of adoption so that war babies would be given opportunities to be adopted abroad.

9.13.3 After the war, the government included a scheme of adoption of war babies by foreigners.[239] Specifically, under the purview of the Bangladesh Abandoned Children (Special

---

[239] 'Rape is a War Crime and those Committed in 1971 should be Tried

Provision) Order of 1972, the then Government stimulated foreign adoption agencies to take war babies from Bangladesh.[240] Consequently, many adoption agencies such as the "US branch of the Geneva-based International Social Service", the "Families for Children (Canada)", the "Kuan-Yin Foundation (Canada)", the "Holt Adoption Program (US)", and "Terre des Hommes (Switzerland)" took the war babies of Bangladesh to Western countries.[241]

9.13.4 Further, the abortion law of Bangladesh was temporarily waived from January to October, 1972 for women who were victims of rape during the war.[242] Moreover, with the direct support of the World Health Organization and the International Planned Parenthood Federation, a Government-mandated victim relief program was introduced to provide abortion facilities to war rape victims.[243] It was reported by one of the doctors involved with this program that approximately 0.17 million abortions of pregnancies resulted from rapes were conducted, while the births of 0.03 million war babies took place during the first 3 months in 1972.[244]

9.13.5 In our survey, out of 19 rape victims who got pregnant due to war time rape, we found that only 6 aborted their conceived children. This is almost one-third of the pregnant rape victims.

---

as such, Argues Kajalie Shehreen Islam,' *The Daily Star*, 5 December 2014.

[240] Bina D'Costa, 'Tragic silence over Bangladesh's babies of war of 1971,' *Himal Southasian*, December 2008, available at <http://www.sacw.net/article581.html> accessed on 25 December 2018.

[241] Ibid.

[242] Nayanika Mookherjee, 'Available Motherhood: Legal Technologies, 'State of Exception' and the Dekinning of 'War Babies' in Bangladesh,' (2007) 14(3) *Journal of Global Child Research* 349.

[243] Amena Mohsin, 'Gendered Nation, Gendered Peace: A Study of Bangladesh,' (2005) *Indian Journal of Gender Studies* 223.

[244] Ibid.

They included Ferdousi (Priyobhashini) Begum of Faridpur district, Romisa Khatun of Mymensingh district, Mollika Ganguly of Barguna district, Sreejita Ray of Patuakhali district, Asma Khatun of Dinajpur district and Mst. Jamila Bewa of Nilphamari district.

9.13.6 However, two third of the pregnant rape victims (i.e. 13 in number) interviewed gave birth to children. They are, Mst. Majeda Begum (Madhobpur) and Heeramoni Shaotal (Chunarughat) of Habiganj district, Bishamuni Bagti and Provarani Malakar (Komolganj) of Moulbhibazaar district, Mukta Bhanu of Daulatpur, Shunamganj district, Elijaan Nesa of Kushtia district, Bokul of Faridpur district, Saleha Begum of Gopalganj district, Safia khatun of Kumilla, Meherun Nahar of Chapainababganj district, Mst. Amina Khatun and Mst. Hapon of Nilphamari district and Tepri Rani Burman of Thakurgaon district.

9.13.7 This research work also found that bringing up war babies has not been an easy task at all. The mother and the war baby, and on certain occasions, the entire family accommodating a war baby faced social ostracism. There were raped mothers who brought up the war babies themselves despite the society. For example, Mukta Bhanu of Daulatpur, Shunamganj district, Bokul of Faridpur district and Tepri Rani Burman of Thakurgaon district looked after their war babies themselves. They had to go through a lot of slights from the society for doing so. They did not have family support as such, but did not remarry to bring up their war babies on their own.

9.13.8 This research project also found that some rape victims giving birth to war babies did receive support from their own families to bring up their children. In many cases, their husbands supported them to accommodate the war babies within the family. For example, the husbands of Heeramoni Shaotal (Chunarughat) of Habiganj district, Bishamuni Bagti and Provarani Malakar

(Komolganj) of Moulbhibazaar district, Mst. Amina Khatun and Mst. Hapon of Nilphamari district accepted the war babies of their wives.

9.13.9 At times, other family members of rape victims surveyed came forward to shoulder the responsibility of bringing up war babies. For example, the war baby (Shamsun Nahar) of Mst. Majeda Begum of Habiganj was brought up and taken care of by Mst. Majeda Begum's own paternal uncle. This uncle also arranged the marriage of the war baby Shamsun Nahar. Even though the rape victim Ms. Tepri Rani Burman of Thakurgaon took up the responsibility of her war baby (Shudhir) on her own, she did get a lot of support from her father while he was alive.

9.13.10 This research project looked at the social treatment given to war babies and his/her rape victim mothers. Society was essentially very cruel in its treatment of war babies. Even though many war babies were given for foreign adoption, the lives of the ones who were left behind in Bangladesh have been quite intolerable. They were subject to constant social slurs and treated as outcastes. They were called names, such as, "Punjabi's Child", "Khan's Child", "Bastard", etc. since their birth.

9.13.11 Furthermore, even when the war baby (Shamsun Nahar) of Mst. Majeda Begum of Habiganj was almost 33 years old and happily married, and the information of her being a war baby reached her in-laws, they started abusing her both physically and mentally for months. At times, they chained her just to show people that she had turned insane and therefore was not capable of continuing with her conjugal life. The husband, finally, divorced her and threw her out of the house for no fault of her own.

9.13.12 Also, war babies remained all through their lives targets of abuse of society. They have not been secure in society. There have always been life threats issued to them in the social culture they grew up. For example, the war baby (Shohodev) of Heeramoni Shaotal (Chunarughat) of Habiganj district was never secure in the vicinity where he grew up. He was ultimately killed at the age of 25.

9.13.13 When the war baby of rape victim Mst. Saleha Begum of Gopalganj district died 4 days after his birth, no one in society actually volunteered to do his death rituals. Painfully, the mother did it on her own and she remembers the incident sadly till date. Many rape victims apprehended the antagonistic treatment their war babies would get and therefore, tried to disown their children. For example, after giving birth to her war baby (a girl), rape victim Safia Khatun of Kumilla district abandoned it in front of someone else's house. Today she feels guilty about the incident but says that she had no other option as there was no one to support her or the baby at that time.

9.14 Trial and its Aftermath

9.14.1 The International Crimes Tribunal of Bangladesh (ICT-BD) turned on the light of justice for people of Bangladesh after almost 40 years by bringing local perpetrators of rape into the court. Many accused persons have been convicted of committing, *inter alia*, the crime of rape of Bengali women in the 1971 war.

9.14.2 The present research projects that all rape victims are satisfied with the ongoing trial of war criminals. They noted that they want the highest punishment *i.e.* death penalty to be awarded to war criminals. However, all rape victims feel that they should be compensated by the war criminals for the crimes committed against them.

9.14.3 Many of them also sought both the government and private facilities for meeting their basic necessities. Their demands mainly include providing them with a decent living place, decent employment for their children and family members, old-age benefit packages on a priority basis, and health care facilities free of cost for the rest of their lives. Some even hope to receive psychological counseling as war rape victims. For example, Kiranbala of Nilphamari district thinks that war rape victims have gone through so much trauma in their lives that there is a need to provide them with mental counseling support.

9.14.4 Many war rape victims (95%) claim that there should be state recognition of war babies. These babies are children of Bengali mothers and therefore there can be no barrier to transmit the nationality to them under the current law. All war rape victims (100%) also demand trial of Pakistani soldiers, which is yet to take place at the ICT-BD. They include Debai and Purathi of Panchgarh district and Laili Begum of Rangpur district.

9.14.5 All (100%) war rape victims would like to see a separate law with strict punishment to be enacted for insulting war rape victims. For example, Azima of Domar of Nilphamari district feels very strongly that the lack of such a law makes war rape victims quite vulnerable in society. To this end, enactment of a prohibitory law is a must for her so that war rape victims can take recourse to the court of law.

9.14.6 It is interesting to note that the survey found that most war rape victims (91%) do not want to be identified or called "*Birangonas*". This feeling is strongly expressed well across the country. For example, Chhyayarun of Sylhet district, Bidya shundori Shutrodhor of Kishoreganj district, Rawshan Ara of Tangail district, Mst. Asma Begum of Kurigram, Amina Khatun of Nilphamari district, are only a few of the women who expressed such sentiment.

9.14.7 Finally, all (100%) of the war rape victims state very strongly that even though the trials of war criminals have bought legal justice to society, they as a group did not get their due share of recognition and respect for the contribution they made for the independence of the country. Their agony has not been reflected in the general narratives of society as it has remained for ages a matter of deliberate national forgetting. Their contribution has also not been narrated in school textbooks. If not individually recognized and respected, at least some sort of murals can be made in every single district of the country so that the new generation is constantly reminded of the contribution war rape victims made during the war of liberation.

10

Conclusion

10.1 To conclude, it can be stated that sexual violence and rape, committed whether during war or peacetime, was widespread and that the women were often victimized by Pakistani men and their collaborators. The experience of the 1971 Liberation War of Bangladesh when perpetrators used the rape of women as a war tactic is hardly discussed in the international arena. However, a growing number of cases recognizing war rape as an illegal act have been taken up partly as a result of the heinous use of rape as a tactic of genocide in both Rwanda and Yugoslavia during 1990s. This study has described various legal mechanisms to hold perpetrators of sexual violence liable under the IHL, the ICHL, decisions in recent war crimes tribunals such as the ICTY, the ICTR, the ICC etc., the *Geneva Convention* IV, the *Genocide Convention*, the *Hague Conventions on the Laws of War etc.*

10.2 Besides, this study shows that the intensive observations of the ICT-BD demonstrated again and again that rape of women was used as a weapon by perpetrators of rape. From the perspectives of Bangladesh, ensuring legal justice is indeed the first step to be taken to redress the wrong done to the victims. The demand of rape victims to get social justice is widespread.

This study would like to conclude that while legal justice has been examples, social justice is still demanded by victims of the 1971 Liberation War in Bangladesh. This study claims that there is ample scope to provide social justice to rape victims in various ways so that they can enjoy complete justice to some extent in their lifetime.

Bibliography

BOOKS

1. A Cassese, *International Law* (New York: Oxford University Press, 6ᵗʰ ed., 2002).

2. A Debnath, 'The Bangladesh Genocide: The Plight of Women' in S Totten (ed), *Plight and Fate of Women During and Following Genocide* (New Brunswick: Transaction Publishers, 2009).

3. A Falguny, *Banglar Nari Songrami: Oitijjher Onusondhan* (Dhaka, Steps Towards Development, 1997).

4. A M A Muhith, *Bangladesh: Emergence of a Nation* (Dhaka, The University Press Limited, 2014).

5. A Mascarronhas, *Bangladesh Rokter Rin* (Dhaka, Hakkani Publishers, 1997).

6. A Nojrul, *Juddhaporadhir Bichar: Jahanara Imamer Chithi* (Dhaka, Anyaprokash, 2009).

7. A Rahman, *Shotrur Matite Muktijuddho* (Dhaka, Agamee Prokashoni, 2009).

8. A Sen, *The Idea of Justice* (England, Penguin Group, 2009).

9. A Sharif, K Nur-Uzzaman and S Kabir (ed), *Ekattorer Ghatok Dalalra Ke Kothay* (Dhaka, Muktijuddho Chetona Bikash Kendro, 1989).

10. A T M Shamsuddin, *Pakistan Jokhon Bhanglo* (Dhaka, The University Press Limited, 2009).

11. B Mohammad, *Swadhin Bangla Betar Kendra* (Dhaka, Anupam Prokashani, 2006).

12. D Das, *Birangona Theke Muktijoddha* (Jessore, Sristy Prokashani, 2015).

13. D Feierstein, *Genocide as Social Pactice: Reorganizing Society under the Nazis and Argentina's Military Juntas* (London, Rutgers University Press, 1st ed., 2014).

14. D Stone (ed), *The Historiography of Genocide* (Palgrave Macmillan, 1st ed, 2008).

15. F A Khan, *Spring 1971: A Centre Stage Account of Bangladesh War of Liberation* (Dhaka, The University Press Limited, 1998).

16. G J A Knoops, *Defenses in Contemporary International Criminal Law* (United States of America: Martinus Nijhoff, 2nd ed., 2007).

17. H Ahmed, *Media and the Liberation War of Bangladesh* vol 3 (Dhaka, Centre for Bangladesh Studies, 2005).

18. H Clarke, *Basic Documents on the International Humanitarian Law: South Asia Collection* (New Delhi,

India: International Committee of the Red Cross, 3rd ed., 2012).

19. H Das, *Smritimoy Ekattor* (Dhaka, Shahittyo Prokash, 2007).

20. H H Rahman (ed), *Bangladesher Shadhinota Juddho: Dolilpotro Vol 5* (Dhaka, Hakkani Publishers, 2009).

21. H Hossain, R Jahan and S Sobhan, *No Better Option?: Industrial Women Workers in Bangladesh* (Dhaka, University Press Limited, 1990).

22. J Nasreen, *Muktijuddhe Sahid Nari* (Dhaka, Anupam Prakashani, 2008).

23. L Collins and D Lapiere, *Freedon at Midnight* (Delhi, Tarang Paperbacks, 1988).

24. M A Hasan and T Degan, *Beyond Denial: The Evidence of a Genocide* (New Millenium 1st ed, 2013).

25. M A Hasan, *Shirsho Ponero Paki Juddhaporadhi* (Dhaka, Somoy Prokashon, 2012).

26. M A K Azad, *India Wins Freedom* (Hyderabad, Orient Longman Limited, 1988).

27. M A Mannan and C S Mannan (ed), *International Documents of Great Liberation War of Bangladesh [1970-71] Vol I* (Dhaka, Jatiya Grontha Prokashan, 2008).

28. M A Mannan and C S Mannan (ed), *International Documents of Great Liberation War of Bangladesh [1970-71] Vol II* (Dhaka, Jatiya Grontha Prokashan, 2008).

29. M A Rashid, *Bangladesher Rajniti: Juddhaparadhi Jamayat Ebong Jongi Proshonga* Vol 1 (Dhaka, Anindya Prokash, 2008).

30. M Chowdhury, *71-er Judhoshishu Obidito Itihash* (Dhaka, Academic Press and Publishers Library, 2015).

31. M Hoque and L E Fletcher (ed), *Colloquium on Accountability of Sexual Violence Crimes and Experiences of the International Tribunals* (Dhaka, Liberation War Museum, 2012).

32. M Hoque, *Gonohottyar Bichare Bongobondhur Oitihashik Bhumika* (Dhaka, Liberation War Museum, 2015).

33. M Hoque, M Alam and S R Mojumdar (ed), *Chhatrochhatrider Songrihito Muktijuddher Protokkhodorshi Vassho* (Dhaka, Liberation War Museum, 2015).

34. M K Jalalzai, *Sectarianism in Pakistan* (Lahore, A. H. Publishers, 1992).

35. M Kishwar, *Off the Beaten Track: Rethinking Gender Justice for Indian Women* (New Delhi, Oxford University Press, 1999).

36. M M Urquhart, *Women of Bengal* (Delhi, Gian Publishing House, 1987).

37. M Mamoon (ed), *Muktijuddher Chinno Dolilpotro* (Dhaka, Ananya, 2011).

38. M Mamoon, *Media and the Liberation War of Bangladesh* vol 2 (Dhaka, Centre for Bangladesh Studies, 2002).

39. M Mamoon, *Sei Sob Pakistani* (Dhaka, The University Press Limited, 2010).

40. M McClymont and S Golub (ed.), *Many Roads to Justice* (United States of America, The Ford Foundation, 2000).

41. M S Alam, *Amar Babar Jibon, Darshon O Dharmochinta* (Dhaka, 2015).

42. N Chowdhury, Hamida A. Begum, Mahmuda Islam, Nazmunnessa Mahtab (ed.), *Women & Politics* (Dhaka, Women for Women, 1994).

43. N Ibrahim, *Ami Birangona Bolchi* (Dhaka, Jagrity Prokashoni, 2010).

44. R Ahmed, *Media and the Liberation War of Bangladesh* vol 1 (Dhaka, Centre for Bangladesh Studies, 2002).

45. R Gallately and B Kiernan, *The Specter of Genocide: Mass Murder in Historical Perspective* (Cambridge University Press, 1st ed, 2003).

46. R Jahan, *The Elusive Agenda: Mainstreaming Women in Development* (Dhaka, University Press Limited, 1995).

47. R Ray, *Fields of Protest: Women's Movements in India* (Minneapolis, University of Minnesota Press, 1999).

48. R Sengupta, *Chitro Sangbadiker Camera-y Muktijuddho* (Dhaka, Shahittyo Prokash, 2016).

49. S Ahmed, A A Chowdhury, R Haider, S Hossain and N U Yusuf (ed), *Ekattorer Chithi* (Dhaka, Prothoma Prokashani, 2013).

50. S Akhtar (ed), *Muktijuddho Poroborti Nari Punorbashon Kendro* (Dhaka, Ain o Shalish Kendra, 2009).

51. S Akhtar, S Begum, M Guhathakurta, H Hossain and S Kamal (ed), *Rising from the Ashes: Women's Narratives of 1971* (Dhaka, The University Press Limited jointly with Ain o Shalish Kendra, 2013).

52. S Akhtar, *Talaash* (Dhaka, Mowla Brothers, 2004).

53. S Brownmiller, *Against Our Will: Men, Women and Rape* (London: Secker & Warburg, 1975).

54. S Brownmiller, *Against Our Will: Men, Women and Rape* (New York: Ballantine Books, 1993).

55. S Hamid, *Why Women Count: Essays on Women in Development in Bangladesh* (Dhaka, The University Press Limited, 1996).

56. S Hossain, *Guerilla O Birangana* (Dhaka, Prothoma Prokashani, 2016).

57. S Kamal, *Ekattorer Diary* (Dhaka, Howlader Prokashoni, 2011).

58. S Khan, *The Fifty Percent: Women in Development and Policy in Bangladesh* (Dhaka, University Press Limited, 1993).

59. S Mostafiz, *Jonochetonay Gonohotta '71* (Dhaka, Pearl Publications, 2013).

60. S Roushon and T Abdullah, *Ekattorer Ognikonna* (Dhaka, Anupom Prokashoni, 1997).

61. S V R Nasr, *The Vanguard of the Islamic Revolution* (California, University of California Press, 1994).

62. Saadullah, *Naari: Audhikar o Ayin* (Dhaka, Somoy Prakashan, 2002).

63. S Usman, *1971: Smritikhondo Mujibnagar* (Dhaka, Somoy Prokashon, 2009).

64. *Sufia Kamal Smarokgrontho* (Dhaka, Sufia Kamal Smarokgrontho Sompadona Porishad, Bangladesh Mohila Parishad, 2011).

65. T Afroz, *Genocide, War Crimes, & Crimes against Humanity in Bangladesh: Trial under International Crimes (Tribunals) Act, 1973* (Forum for Secular Bangladesh and Trials of War Criminals of 1971, 1st ed, 2010).

66. *Uniform Family Code* (Dhaka, Bangladesh Mohila Parishad, 1993).

67. V Olsen and J Lockerbie, *Daktar: Diplomat in Bangladesh* (Chicago, USA, Moody Publishers, 1973).

68. W A Schabas, *An Introduction to the International Criminal Court* (Cambridge University Press, 4th ed., 2011).

69. W A Schabas, *Genocide in International: The Crime of Crimes* (Cambridge University Press, 2nd ed, 2009).

70. W A Schabas, *The UN International Criminal Tribunals: The Former Yugoslavia, Rwanda and Sierra Leon* (New York: Cambridge University Press, 1st ed., 2006).

71. W B Milam, *Bangladesh and Pakistan: Flirting with Failure in South Asia* (Dhaka, The University Press Limited, 2010).

JOURNAL ARTICLES

1. A M Chenoy, 'Women in the South Asian Conflict Zones' (2004) 11(35) *South Asian Survey* 19.

2. A Mohsin, 'Gendered Nation, Gendered Peace: A Study of Bangladesh,' (2005) *Indian Journal of Gender Studies* 223.

3. A Saha, 'Rape as a War Crime: The Position of International Law since World War II' (2009) 2 *J. E. Asia & Int'l L.* 497.

4. B Nowrojee, 'Making the Invisible War Crime Visible: Post-Conflict Justice for Sierra Leone's Rape Victims' (2005) 18 *Harv. Hum Rts. J.* 85.

5. C J Smith, 'History of Rape and Rape Laws' (1974) 60 *Women Law. J.* 188.

6. *CEDAW Benchbook* (Dhaka, Ministry of Law, Justice and Parliamentary Affairs, 2013).

7. E J Wood, 'Rape is Not Inevitable in War' (2010) 5 *Yale J. Int'l Aff.* 161.

8. K Cleary and S Sacouto, 'The Importance of Effective Investigation of Sexual Violence and Gender-Based Crimes at the International Criminal Court' (2009) 17 *American University Journal of Gender Social Policy and Law* 337.

9. K G Neill, 'Duty, Honour, Rape: Sexual Assault against Women during War' (November 2000) 2(1) *Journal of International Women's Studies,* Bridgewater State College 23.

10. K Parker and J F Chew, 'Compensation for Japan's World War H War-Rape Victims' (1993-94) 17 *Hastings Int'l & Comp. L. Rev.* 497.

11. L A Fairstein, 'Sexual Violence. Our War against Rape' (1994) 5 *Md. J. Contemp. Legal Issues* 173.

12. L Mokhtanzadeh, 'Ending War Rape: A Matter of Cumulative Convictions' (2013) 36 *Fordham Int'l L.J.* 1021.

13. L Sharlach, *'Rape as Genocide: Bangladesh, the Former Yugoslavia, and Rwanda'* (2000) 22(1) *New Political Science* 413.

14. M Hoque and U Wara (ed), *Bangladesh Genocide and the Issue of Justice* (Dhaka, Liberation War Museum, 2013).

15. M Hoque and U Wara (ed), *From Genocide to Justice: National and Global Perspective* (Dhaka, Liberation War Museum, 2014).

16. M Morris, 'By Force of Arms: Rape, War, And Military Culture' (1995-96) 45 *Duke L.J.* 651.

17. N Mookherjee, 'Available Motherhood: Legal Technologies, 'State of Exception' and the Dekinning of 'War Babies' in Bangladesh,' (2007) 14(3) *Journal of Global Child Research* 349.

18. N Mookherjee, 'Bangladesh War of 1971: A Prescription for Reconciliation?' (2006) 41(36) *Economic and Political Weekly* 3901.

19. P H Davis, 'The Politics of Prosecuting Rape as a War Crime' (2000) 34 *Int'l L.* 1223.

20. R J Goldstone, 'Prosecuting Rape as a War Crime' (2002) 34 *Case W. Res. J. Int'l L.* 277.

21. S Rahman and C Baxter, 'Historical Dictionary of Bangladesh,' (2002) *Scarecrow* 1, 52.

22. S Swiss and J Giller, 'Rape as a Crime of War: A Medical Perspective' (August 1993) 270 *Journal of the American Medical Association* (USA) 612.

23. T L Tompkins, 'Prosecuting Rape as a War Crime: Speaking the Unspeakable' (1994-95) 70 *Notre Dame L. Rev.* 845.

CASES

- **Bangladesh**

1. *Ali Ahsan Muhammad Mujahid vs. The Chief Prosecutor*, ICT-BD, Criminal Review Petition 62/2015.

2. *Ali Ahsan Muhammad Mujahid vs. The Chief Prosecutor*, ICT-BD, Criminal Appeal (A) 103/2013.

3. *Allama Delwar Hossain Sayedee vs. The Government of the People's Republic of Bangladesh, represented by the Chief Prosecutor*, ICT-BD, Criminal Appeal (A) 39/2013.

4. *Mir Quasem Ali vs. The Chief Prosecutor*, ICT-BD, Criminal Appeal (A) 144/2014.

5. *Motiur Rahman Nizami vs. The Chief Prosecutor*, ICT-BD, Criminal Review Petition 42/2016.

6. *Motiur Rahman Nizami vs. The Government of Bangladesh,* represented by the Chief Prosecutor, ICT-BD, Criminal Appeal (A) 143/2014.

7. *Salauddin Qader Chowdhury vs. The Chief Prosecutor,* ICT-BD, Bangladesh, Criminal Appeal No.122 of 2013.

8. *Salauddin Qader Chowdhury vs. The Chief Prosecutor,* ICT-BD, Criminal Review Petition No.63 of 2015.

9. *The Chief Prosecutor vs. (1) Ashrafuzzaman Khan @ Naeb Ali Khan & (2) Chowdhury Mueen Uddin,* ICT-BD 01 of 2013.

10. *The Chief Prosecutor vs. A.T.M Azharul Islam,* ICT-BD 05 of 2013.

11. *The Chief Prosecutor vs. Abdul Quader Molla,* ICT-BD 02 of 2012.

12. *The Chief Prosecutor vs. Ali Ahsan Muhammad Mujahid,* ICT-BD 04 of 2012.

13. *The Chief Prosecutor vs. Delowar Hossain Sayeedi,* ICT-BD 01 of 2011.

14. *The Chief Prosecutor vs. Md. Abdul Alim @ M.A Alim,* ICT-BD 01 of 2012.

15. *The Chief Prosecutor vs. Md. Abdul Jabbar Engineer,* ICT-BD 01 of 2014.

16. *The Chief Prosecutor vs. Md. Forkan Mallik @ Forkan* ICT-BD 03 of 2014.

17. *The Chief Prosecutor vs. Md. Mahidur Rahman & Md. Afsar Hossain @ Chutu*, ICT-BD 02 of 2014.

18. *The Chief Prosecutor vs. Md. Mobarak Hossain @ Mobarak Ali*, ICT-BD 01 of 2013.

19. *The Chief Prosecutor vs. Md. Obaidul Haque alias Taher, and Ataur Rahman alias Noni*, ICT-BD 04 of 2014.

20. *The Chief Prosecutor vs. Mir Quasem Ali*, ICT-BD 03 of 2013.

21. *The Chief Prosecutor vs. Mohibur Rahman alias Boro Mia, Mujibur Rahman alias Angur Mia and Md. Abdur Razzak*, ICT-BD 03 of 2015.

22. *The Chief Prosecutor vs. Motiur Rahman Nizami*, ICT-BD 03 of 2011.

23. *The Chief Prosecutor vs. Moulana Abdul Kalam Azad*, ICT-BD 05 of 2012.

24. *The Chief Prosecutor vs. Moulana Abdus Sobhan*, ICT-BD 01 of 2014.

25. *The Chief Prosecutor vs. Muhammad Kamaruzzaman*, ICT-BD 03 of 2012.

26. *The Chief Prosecutor vs. Professor Ghulam Azam*, ICT-BD 06 of 2011.

27. *The Chief Prosecutor vs. Salauddin Quader Chowdhury*, ICT-BD 02 of 2011.

28. *The Chief Prosecutor vs. Shamsuddin Ahmed, Gazi Md. Abdul Mannan, Nasiruddin Ahmed alias Md. Nasir alias*

Captain ATM Nasir, Md. Hafizuddin and Md. Azharul Islam, ICT-BD 01 of 2015.

29. *The Chief Prosecutor vs. Sheikh Sirajul Haque alias Siraj Master, Khan Akram Hossain and Abdul Latif Talukder (now dead),* ICT-BD 03 of 2014.

30. *The Chief Prosecutor vs. Syed Md. Hachhan alias Syed Md. Hasan alias Hachhen, Ali* ICT-BD 02 of 2014.

31. *The Chief Prosecutor vs. Syed Md. Qaiser,* ICT-BD 04 of 2013.

32. *The Chief Prosecutor vs. Zahid Hossain Khokon @ M.A. Zahid @ Khokon Matubbar @ Khokon,* ICT-BD 04 of 2013.

- **Other Jurisdictions**

1. *Aloys Simba v. The Prosecutor* (ICTR-01-76-A, Appeals Chamber, 27 November 2007).

2. *Eliézer Niyitegeka v. The Prosecutor* (ICTR-96-14-A, Appeals Chamber, 9 July 2004).

3. *Emmanuel Ndindabahizi v. The Prosecutor* (ICTR-2001-71-A, Appeals Chamber, 16 January 2007).

4. *Ferdinand Nahimana, Jean-Bosco Barayagwiza and Hassan Ngeze v. The Prosecutor* (ICTR-99-52-A, Appeals Chamber, 28 November 2007).

5. *Georges Anderson Nderubumwe Rutaganda v. The Prosecutor* (ICTR-96-3-A, Appeals Chamber, 26 May 2003).

6. *Sylvestre Gacumbitsi v. The Prosecutor* (ICTR-2001-64-A, Appeals Chamber, 7 July 2006).

7. *The Prosecutor v. Drazen Erdemović* (ICTY 96-22-A, Appeals Chamber, 7 October 1997).

8. *The Prosecutor v. Laurent Semanza* (ICTR-97-20-T, Trial Chamber, 15 May 2003).

9. *The Prosecutor v. Al Bashir* (ICC-02/05-01/09, Pre-Trial Chamber I).

10. *The Prosecutor v. Alfred Musema* (ICTR-96-13-A, Appeals Chamber, 27 January 2000).

11. *The Prosecutor v. Aloys Simba* (ICTR-01-76-T, Trial Chamber, 13 December 2005).

12. *The Prosecutor v. André Ntagerura, Emmanuel Bagambiki and Samuel Imanishimwe* (ICTR-99-46-T, Trial Chamber, 25 February 2004).

13. *The Prosecutor v. Athanase Seromba* (ICTR-2001-66-T, Trial Chamber, 13 December 2006).

14. *The Prosecutor v. Brima et. al.* ('AFRC' Case) (SCSL-04-16-T, Trial Chamber, 20 June 2007 & SCSL-2004-16-A, Appeals Chamber, 22 February 2008).

15. *The Prosecutor v. Clement Kayishema and Obed Ruzindana* (ICTR-95-1-T, Trial Chamber, 21 May 1999).

16. *The Prosecutor v. Dario Kordic, and Mario Cerkez* (ICTY-95-14/2-T, Trial Chamber, 26 February 2001).

17. *The Prosecutor v. Dominic Ongwen* (ICC-02/04-01/15, Pre-Trial Chamber II).

18. *The Prosecutor v. Dragoljub Kunarak, Radomir Kovak and Zoran Vukovic (ICTY-96-23-T & 23/1-T, Trial Chamber, 22 February 2001).*

19. *The Prosecutor v. Emmanuel Ndindabahizi* (ICTR-2001-71-T, Trial Chamber, 15 July 2004).

20. *The Prosecutor v. Ferdinand Nahimana, Jean-Bosco Barayagwiza and Hassan Ngeze* (ICTR-99-52-T, Trial Chamber, 3 December 2003).

21. *The Prosecutor v. Furundzija* (ICTY-95-17/1-T, Trial Chamber, 10 December 1998).

22. *The Prosecutor v. Goran Jelisić* (ICTY-95-10-A, Appeal Chamber, 5 July 2001).

23. *The Prosecutor v. Goran Jelisić* (ICTY-95-10-T, Trial Chamber, 14 December 1999).

24. *The Prosecutor v. Jean de Dieu Kamuhanda* (ICTR-95-54A-T, Trial Chamber, 22 January 2004).

25. *The Prosecutor v. Jean Mpambara* (ICTR-01-65-T, Trial Chamber, 11 September 2006).

26. *The Prosecutor v. Jean-Paul Akayesu* (ICTR-96-4-T, Trial Chamber, 2 September 1998).

27. *The Prosecutor v. Jean-Paul Akayesu* (ICTR-96-4-T, Trial Chamber, 2 September 1998).

28. *The Prosecutor v. Jean-Pierre Bemba Gombo* (ICC-01/05/-01/08-3343, Trial Chamber III).

29. *The Prosecutor v. Juvénal Kajelijeli* (ICTR- 98-44A-T, Trial Chamber, 1 December 2003).

30. *The Prosecutor v. Katanga & Chui* (ICC-01/04-01/07, Decision on the Confirmation of Charges, 30 September 2008.

31. *The Prosecutor v. Kvocka* (ICTY-98-30/I-T, Trial Chamber, 2 November 2001).

32. *The Prosecutor v. Mikaeli Muhimana* (ICTR- 95-1B-T, Trial Chamber, 28 April 2005).

33. *The Prosecutor v. Milomir Stakic* (ICTY-97-24-T, Trial Chamber, 31 July 2003).

34. *The Prosecutor v. Popovic* (ICTY-05-88-T, Trial Chamber, 10 June 2010).

35. *The Prosecutor v. Radislav Krstic* (ICTY-98-33-A, Appeals Chamber, 19 April 2004).

36. *The Prosecutor v. Radoslav Brdjanin* (ICTY-99-36-T, Trial Chamber, 1 September 2004).

37. *The Prosecutor v. Semanza* (ICTR-97-20, Trial Chamber, 15 May 2003).

38. *The Prosecutor v. Sesay et. al.* ('RUF' Case) (SCSL-04-15-T, Trial Chamber, 2 March 2009).

39. *The Prosecutor v. Sikirica et al.* (ICTY-95-8-T, Trial Chamber, 13 November 2001).

40. *The Prosecutor v. Siméon Nchamihigo* (ICTR-01-63-T, Trial Chamber, 12 November 2008).

41. *The Prosecutor v. Sylvestre Gacumbitsi* (ICTR-2001-64-T, Trial Chamber, 17 June 2004).

42. *The Prosecutor v. Tharcisse Muvunyi* (ICTR-2000-55 A-T, Trial Chamber 12 September, 2006).

43. *The Prosecutor v. Theoneste Bagosora et al* (ICTR-98-41-T, Trial Chamber, 18 December 2008).

44. *The Prosecutor v. Thomas Lubanga Dyilo* (ICC-01/04-01/06).

45. *The Prosecutor v. Thomas Lubanga Dyilo* (ICC-01/04-01/06, Trial Chamber I).

46. *The Prosecutor v. Vidoje Blagojevic and Dragan Jokic* (ICTY-02-60-T, Trial Chamber, 17 January 2005).

47. *The Prosecutor v. Zejnil Delalid ('Celebidi')* (ICTY-96-21-A, Appeals Chamber, 20 February 2001).

NEWSPAPER ARTICLES

1. 'High Powered Body to Rehabilitate Women Victims', *The Bangladesh Observer*, 24 February 1972.

2. 'The World: East Pakistan: East Pakistan: Even the Skies Weep', *Time Magazine*, 25 October 1971.

3. A Astrachan, 'U.N. Asked to Aid Bengali Abortions', *The Washington Post*, 22 March 1972.

4. A Menen, 'The Rape of Bangladesh', *The New York Times*, 23 July 1972.

5. Associated Press, 'Killing of Babies Feared in Bengal', *The New York Times*, 5 March 1972.

6. G Greer, 'The Rape of the Bengali Women', *The Sunday Times*, April 9 1972.

7. K S Islam, 'Healing the Hidden Wounds of War' 4(12) *The Daily Star (Forum)*, Dhaka, December 2010.

8. N Mookherjee, 'Skewing the History of Rape in 1971', 1(2) *Daily Star Forum*, December 2006.

OTHERS

1. *'Broken Bodies, Broken Dreams: Violence Against Women Exposed'*, United Nations OCHA/IRIN Publication, 2005.

2. A Ahmed, 'Bangladesh 1971: War Crimes, Genocide and Crimes against Humanity- Operation Search Light: The Targets', conference paper presented at the Bangladesh Study Group programme at Kean University entitled *Bangladesh 1971: Addressing Claims of War Crimes, Genocide and Crimes against Humanity*, 18 October 2009.

3. H H Rahman, *Bangladesher Shadhinota Juddho: Dolilpotro, Oshtom Khondo* (History of Bangladesh War of Independence: Documents, Vol-8) (Dhaka: Ministry of Information, 1984).

4. *Hamoodur Rahman Commission Report*, Cabinet Secretariat, Government of Pakistan, Rawalpindi, 25 May 1974.

5. L Jefferson, 'In War as In Peace: Sexual Violence and Women's Status', (Human Rights Watch).

6. L Kelly, 'Wars Against Women: Sexual Violence, Sexual Politics and the Militarised State in S Jacobs, R Jacobson and J Marchbank (eds) *States of Conflict: Gender, Violence and Resistance* (London: Zed Books, 2001).

7. M Guhathakurta, *Dhorshon Ekti Juddhaporadh* (Rape is a War Crime), (Dhaka: Bulletin of Ain-O-Shalish Kendra, 1996).

8. M Hoque and L E Flecher, *Colloquium on Accountability of Sexual Violence Crimes and Experiences of the International Tribunals* (Dhaka: Liberation War Museum, 2012).

9. N Ibrahim, *Ami Birangona Bolchi* (This is the 'War-Heroine' Speaking), 2 Volumes (Dhaka: Jagriti, 1994-5).

10. N Mookherjee, 'A Lot of History: Sexual Violence, Public Memories and the Bangladesh Liberation War of 1971', Ph. D. Thesis (London: School of Oriental and African Studies, University of London, 2002).

11. R Seifert, 'War and Rape: Analytical Approaches', paper presented at the Women's International League for Peace and Freedom, Switzerland in April 1993.

12. S Kabir, *Tormenting Seventy One: An account of Pakistan Army's Atrocities during Bangladesh Liberation War of 1971* (Dhaka: Nirmul Committee, 2006).

13. S Akhtar, S Begum, H Hossain, S Kamal and M Guhathakurta, (eds), *Narir Ekattor O Juddhoporoborti Koththo Kahini* (Oral History Accounts of Women's

Experiences During 1971 and After the War), (Dhaka: Ain-O-Shalish-Kendro, 2001).

14. S Bose, 'Anatomy of Violence: Analysis of Civil War in East Pakistan in 1971', *Economic and Political Weekly*, 8 October 2005.

15. S R Khan, 'To the Victor Go the Spoils: Wartime Rape on Trial' in T Afroz (ed) *Genocide, War Crimes & Crimes Against Humanity in Bangladesh: Trial under International Crimes (Tribunals) Act, 1973* (Dhaka: Forum for Secular Bangladesh and Trial of War Criminals of 1971, 2010).

16. Secretary-General Kofi Annan, United Nations Day for Women's Rights and International Peace, 6 March 2000.

17. Special Rapporteur on Violence against Women in the November 1994 ECOSOC Report numbered E/CN.4/1995/42 presented at the fiftieth session of the Commission on Human Rights, at paragraph 271(a).

18. *Women and War*, directed by T Masud and C masud, produced by Ain-O-Shalish-Kendra and Audiovision (2000); *Tahader Juddho* (Their War) directed by A Choudhury (2001).

19. Y Saikia, 'Overcoming the Silent Archive in Bangladesh: Women Bearing Witness to Violence in the 1971 Liberation' War in M Skidmore and P Lawrence (eds).

Annexure 1

Survey

Name... Age.........................

District of origin? .... Religion....................

Current district? ....

Do you now have a husband?..

How many children do you have?...

Who do you live with now?...

....

Educational qualification?..

Yes √ **No X**

	Information related Sexual Torture	
1	How old were you in 1971?	
2	Were you married then?	
3	If married, did you have any child then?	
4	How many children did you have then?	
5	Were you sexually tortured in your house in 1971?	
6	Were you sexually tortured in any torture camp in 1971?	
7	For how long were you sexually tortured in 1971?	
8	Did you receive any government or private medical treatment after the sexual violence in 1971?	
9	Are you aware of sexual violence of any young boy in 1971?	
	Information related to Family and Social Attitude	
10	Did your family accept you back after the sexual violence of 1971?	
11	If yes, then whether the attitude of the male members of your family towards you sympathetic?	
12	If yes, then whether the attitude of the female members of your family towards you sympathetic?	
13	After becoming the victim of sexual violence in 1971, did the society disrespect or insult you?	
14	If yes, then whether the people in the society used abusive language towards you?	
15	Does your daughter-in-law disrespect or insult you for becoming the victim of sexual violence in 1971?	
16	Does your son-in-law disrespect or insult you for becoming the victim of sexual violence in 1971?	

17	Do the in-laws families of your children disrespect or insult you for becoming the victim of sexual violence in 1971?	
18	Do the in-laws families of your children disrespect or insult your children for you becoming the victim of sexual violence in 1971?	
19	If your family did not accept you back after the sexual violence of 1971, where did you go or live?	
20	If your family did not accept you back after the sexual violence of 1971, did they keep contact with you?	

Information relating to Financial Conditions

21	How did you financially sustain after becoming the victim of sexual violence in 1971?	
22	After becoming the victim of sexual violence in 1971, did you receive any financial support from the government?	
23	After becoming the victim of sexual violence in 1971, did you receive any financial support from the private sector?	

Information relating to Re-marriage

24	If you were unmarried before becoming the victim of sexual violence in 1971, did you get married later on?	
25	If you were married before becoming the victim of sexual violence in 1971, did you go back to your husband?	
26	If your earlier hhusband declined to accept you, did you get married again?	
27	Was the new husband already married?	
28	Did the new husband have another wife?	
29	What was the age difference between you and your new husband?	

30	Did the new husband or his family members disrespect or insult you for becoming the victim of sexual torture in 1971?	

Information relating to the Trial

31	Do you want trials of the perpetrators who had committed sexual violence in 1971?	
32	Are you happy for the fact that the government has initiated the trial of sexual violence perpetrators after almost 40 years of the 1971 war?	
33	Do you believe that these trials would ensure justice to the victims of sexual violence committed in 1971?	
34	What do you think should be the proper punishment of the prepetrators of sexual violence committed in 1971?	
35	Do you think that the perpetrators of sexual violence committed in 1971 should be made to pay reparation to the victims?	
36	Do you think that the attitude towards the victims of sexual violence committed in 1971 has changed after these trials?	
37	According to you, what more could be done for the victims of sexual violence committed in 1971 by the society and the State? • providing free medical treatment • providing financial support • providing housing • building sculpture in every district to facilitate social recogniton • awarding certificate as freedom fighters • inclusion of the history of sacrifice of the victims of sexual violence committed in 1971 in the school text books • others:	

Information relating to War Babies	
38	Did you become pregnant due to the sexual violence of 1971?	
39	If yes, did you abort the child?	
40	If not, then when was the child born?	
41	What was the gender of the child?	
42	Who brought up the child?	
43	Was the child accepted by your new husband and his family?	
44	Have your family been sympathetic towards the child?	
45	Has the society been sympathetic towards the child?	
46	Did the society disrespect or insult the child?	
47	Did the society use abusive language towards the child?	

Annexure 2

List Of Interviewees

BARISHAL	Barishal	1	Nurjahan Begum
	Barguna	2	Amina Khatun
		3	Anima Ganguli
		4	Horidashi Ghosh
		5	Jomila Khatun
		6	Mollika Ganguli
		7	Putul Rani Roy
		8	Smriti Dashi Ghosh
	Bhola		
	Jhalokathi	9	Asha Rani Mondol
		10	Shobita Rani Dhar
		11	Shova Rani Das
		12	Shyamoli Pal
		13	Fulburu Begum
		14	Hajera Khatun
		15	Jamila Khatun
		16	Joyful Banu
		17	Monowara
		18	Monowara Begum

	Patuakhali	19	Moumita Rani Bala
		20	Mst. Aleya Begum
		21	Mst. Aliya Begum
		22	Pijita Ray
		23	Rizia Begum
		24	Shova Rani Karmakar (1)
		25	Shova Rani Karmakar (2)
		26	Shushoma Karmakar
		27	Srijita Ray
	Pirojpur	28	Nazma Begum
		29	Shova Kar
		30	Shuruchi Rani Shaha
CHITTAGONG	Bandarban		
	Brahmanbaria	31	Rezia Begum
	Chandpur	32	Honufa Begum
	Chittagong	33	Amena Begum
		34	Amena Khatun (1)
		35	Amena Khatun (2)
		36	Amena Khatun (3)
		37	Anowara Begum (1)
		38	Anowara Begum (2)
		39	Apia Khatun
		40	Bhanumoti Das
		41	Bibi Kulsum
		42	Bokul Rani De
		43	Delwara Begum
		44	Fazarer Nesa
		45	Firoza Khatun
		46	Halima Begum
		47	Haradhon Bibi
		48	Hazera Khatun
		49	Hosne Ara
		50	Jahanara Begum
		51	Jahera Begum

	52	Jharna	
	53	Joleikha Begum	
	54	Jyotsna Begum	
	55	Kadarer Nesa	
	56	Kanchan Mala	
	57	Khadija Begum	
	58	Minu Das	
	59	Monowara	
	60	Monowara Begum	
	61	Moriom Bibi (1)	
	62	Moriom Bibi (2)	
	63	Mst. Shurma Khatun	
	64	Mst. Zamina Khatun	
	65	Nojum Bia	
	66	Noorjahan Begum	
	67	Ofula Khatun	
	68	Rawshan Ara Begum	
	69	Saleha Bibi	
	70	Shabitri Das	
	71	Shorifa Begum	
	72	Sofura Khatun	
	73	Sokhina Khatun	
	74	Sufia Begum (1)	
	75	Sufia Begum (2)	
	76	Tahera	
	77	Torikunnesa	
	78	Zohra Khatun	
Comilla	79	Aleya (Anu)	
	80	Safiya Khatun	
Cox's Bazar			
Khagrachhari	81	Cheng Sama Mogh	
	82	Hola Mraso Aung Marma	
Lakshmipur	83	Hazera Khatun	
Feni	84	Monowara	

	Noakhali	85	Ankurer Nesa
		86	Hasina Begum
		87	Monsura Khatun
	Rangamati	88	Jharna Das
		89	Meera Rani Barua
		90	Noorjahan Begum
		91	Rashida Debi Chakma
DHAKA	Dhaka	92	Honufa Khatun
		93	Momena Begum
		94	Rawshan Ara Begum
	Faridpur	95	Bokul
		96	Beauty Begum
		97	Ferdousi (Priyobhashini) Begum
	Gazipur	98	Shoilo Bala Das
		99	Momtaz Begum
	Gopalganj	100	Laili Begum
		101	Meera Banik
		102	Mst. Saleha Begum
		103	Nazma Begum (Kakon
		104	Bala)
		105	Rawshan Ara
			Shuruchi Bishwash
	Kishoreganj	106	Bhanumoti Shutrodhor
		107	Bidya Shundori Shutrodhor
		108	Komola Bormon
		109	Razia Khatun
		110	Rashmoni Chakrabarty
		111	Shobha Rani Shutrodhor
		112	Shomola Bormon
	Madaripur		
	Manikganj		
	Munshiganj	113	Kanchan Mala
	Narayanganj	114	Lokhkhi Rani Pal
		115	Romola Devi

	Narsingdi	116	Jyotsna Begum
		117	Kona Rani Das
		118	Rezia Begum
		119	Shahzadi Begum
		120	Shorifa Khatun
	Rajbari	121	Rizia Khatun
	Shariatpur	122	Ananta Bala Pal
		123	Anjali Malo
		124	Anju
		125	Arati
		126	Banu Bibi
		127	Bijoya Malo
		128	Jharna Bala Dey
		129	Jogomaya Malo
		130	Jyotsna
		131	Kamala
		132	Minoti Bala Poddar
		133	Modhu Bala Dey
		134	Ramala Dey
		135	Shumitra
		136	Toruni Devi
		137	Usha Malo
	Tangail	138	Bhakti Rani Pal
		139	Bhanu Begum
		140	Rawshan Ara
KHULNA	Bagerhat	141	Ayesha Khatun
		142	Meherjan Khatun
		143	Roison (Suraiya Begum)
	Chuadanga		
	Jessore	144	Ashura Khatun
	Jhinaidah		
	Khulna	145	Fulera Begum
		146	Gurudashi Mondol

	Kushtia	147	Dulzan Nesa
		148	Elizan Nesa (1)
		149	Elizan Nesa (2)
		150	Masuda Khatun
		151	Momena Khatun (1)
		152	Momena Khatun (2)
	Magura	153	Lokhkhi Rani
	Meherpur		
	Narail	154	Bela Rani Ghosh
	Satkhira	155	Jolekha Khatun
		156	Roison Bibi
MYMENSINGH	Jamalpur	157	Asiron Begum
	Mymensingh	158	Bashonti Rani Rishi
		159	Gita Rani Rishi
		160	Moymona Khatun
		161	Nirmola Rishi
		162	Noorjahan (1)
		163	Noorjahan (2)
		164	Poribin Nesa Bibi
		165	Romesa Khatun
		166	Shurbala Singh
		167	Zahira Khatun
	Netrokona	168	Jyotsna Rani
		169	Mst. Kanchan Mala
		170	Roma Boti Bose
	Sherpur	171	Asiron
		172	Hafiza Bewa
		173	Hasena Banu
		174	Jobeda Bewa (1)
		175	Jobeda Bewa (2)
		176	Korfuly Bewa
		177	Mst. Hachhen Banu
		178	Shomola Bewa
RAJSHAHI	Bogra		

Chapainawabganj	179	Meherunnahar
	180	Mst. Razakunnesa
	181	Mst. Shamsun Nahar
	182	Mst. Shareefa Khatun
	183	Nazma Khatun
	184	Roza Begum
Joypurhat		
Naogaon	185	Bani Bala Pal
	186	Kali Rani Pal
	187	Khanto Bala Pal
	188	Mayabala Shutrodhar
	189	Rashmoni Shutrodhar
	190	Renu Bala Pal
	191	Shondhya Rani Pal
	192	Shushoma Bala Shutrodhar
	193	Shushoma Pal
Natore	194	Johura Begum
Pabna		
Rajshahi	195	Latifa Begum
	196	Parul Begum
	197	Shurjan
	198	Shova
Sirajganj	199	Asia Begum (1)
	200	Asia Begum (2)
	201	Aymona Begum
	202	Aysha Begum
	203	Bahaton Bewa
	204	Hajera Khatun
	205	Hamida Begum
	206	Hasina Bewa
	207	Joygun Begum
	208	Jyotsna Banu
	209	Komola Begum

		210	Korimon Begum
		211	Mahela Bewa
		212	Monu Kundu
		213	Mst. Shamsun Nahar
		214	Begum
		215	Noorjahan
		216	Rahila Begum
		217	Rahima Bewa
		218	Raju Bala De
		219	Samina Khatun
		220	Shurjo Begum
			Suraiya Begum (Dhuli)
RANGPUR	Dinajpur	221	Asma Khatun
		222	Mst. Morzina Begum
	Gaibanda	223	Fulmoti Rani Robidas
		224	Shonaban
	Kurigram	225	Mst. Abiron Bibi
		226	Mst. Aklima Begum
		227	Mst. Ambia Begum
		228	Mst. Amena Begum
		229	Mst. Asia Bewa
		230	Mst. Asma Begum
		231	Mst. Aysha Begum
		232	Mst. Bosiron Begum
		233	Mst. Bulbuli Rani
		234	Mst. Dolo Bewa
		235	Mst. Fatema Begum (1)
		236	Mst. Fatema Begum (2)
		237	Mst. Fatema Begum (3)
		238	Mst. Gendi Bewa
		239	Mst. Hasina Begum
		240	Mst. Hazera Begum
		241	Mst. Jarina Khatun
		242	Mst. Khairun Begum

243	Mst. Khoteja Begum (1)
244	Mst. Khoteja Begum (2)
245	Mst. Khuki Begum
246	Mst. Kobila Begum
247	Mst. Kosvan Begum
248	Mst. Maleka Begum
249	Mst. Meherjan (1)
250	Mst. Meherjan (2)
251	Mst. Meherun Nesa
252	Mst. Mojida Begum
253	Mst. Mollika Begum (1)
254	Mst. Mollika Begum (2)
255	Mst. Morium Bewa
256	Mst. Moyna Begum
257	Mst. Moyna Bewa
258	Mst. Nesamon Begum
259	Mst. Nosimon Bewa
260	Mst. Poniron Begum
261	Mst. Rani Begum
262	Mst. Rezia Khatun
263	Mst. Rohima Begum
264	Mst. Rohima Khatun
265	Mst. Rupban Bewa
266	Mst. Sahera Begum
267	Mst. Saheron Bibi
268	Mst. Saleha Begum
269	Mst. Saleha Bewa
270	Mst. Shamsun Nahar
271	Mst. Shobjaan Begum
272	Mst. Shurujjon Bewa
273	Mst. Tokiron
274	Mst. Toru Bala Roy
275	Mst. Zaheda Begum

Lalmonirhat	276	Khaleya Bewa
	277	Khotina Begum
	278	Monowara Begum
	279	Mst. Khotiza
	280	Mst. Ramisa
	281	Saleha Khatun
Nilphamari	282	Ajima
	283	Gyanoda Bormoni
	284	Jamila Begum
	285	Kiron Bala
	286	Mst. Amina Khatun
	287	Mst. Asia Khatun
	288	Mst. Ayesha Begum
	289	Mst. Begum Ara
	290	Mst. Eziron Begum
	291	Mst. Hapon
	292	Mst. Jamila Bewa
	293	Mst. Jomila Begum
	294	Mst. Korima Begum
	295	Mst. Momtaz Begum
	296	Mst. Morjina Begum (1)
	297	Mst. Morjina Begum (2)
	298	Mst. Morjina Begum (3)
	299	Mst. Rahima Khatun
	300	Mst. Rokeya Begum
	301	Mst. Rokeya Khatun
	302	Mst. Zaheda Begum
	303	Mst. Zahera Begum
	304	Mst. Zohra Khatun
	305	Nobiya Begum
	306	Nolita Rani
	307	Nurjahan
	308	Ojifa
	309	Sabiya

	310	Shorifa
	311	Shyamla Bala
	312	Sohiron
	313	Somari Begum
	314	Zorina Begum
Panchgarh	315	Apela Begum
	316	Debai
	317	Purathi
	318	Zorifon
Rangpur	319	Anwara Begum
	320	Layli Begum
	321	Mst. Monsura Khatun
Thakurgaon	322	Amena Begum
	323	Amina Begum
	324	Chanmoni Sokhina
	325	Chitto Bala
	326	Hafeza Begum
	327	Hanufa Begum
	328	Hasina Begum
	329	Jamela Khatun
	330	Jharna Rani Mondol
	331	Jobeda Bewa
	332	Maleka Begum
	333	Moni Kisku
	334	Mortuza Khatun
	335	Mst. Rezia Begum
	336	Mst. Romesa Begum
	337	Muklesa Begum
	338	Noorjahan Begum
	339	Rabeya Bewa
	340	Sheeta Hemran
	341	Shumi Rashugi
	342	Sreemoti Tirtha Bala
	343	Tepri Rani Barman

SYLHET (4)	Habiganj	344	Abeda Khatun
		345	Abeda Khatun Akshi
		346	Budhuni Urang
		347	Chhabeda
		348	Jolika Begum
		349	Mondo Tanti
		350	Mosammat Majeda Begum
		351	Moymona Bibi
		352	Pushpo Rani Boidyo
		353	Shabitri Nayek
		354	Tarabanu
	Moulvibazar	355	Arina
		356	Bishamuni Bagti
		357	Boishakhi Bunarji
		358	Fulbashia Chasha
		359	Heeramoni Shaontal
		360	Janki Tanti
		361	Monowara
		362	Nidra Bunarji
		363	Probashi Malakar
		364	Probha Rani Malakar
		365	Safia Khatun
		366	Shobita Bagti
		367	Shondhya Rani Deb
		368	Shottoboti Ghashi
		369	Shuvodra Bunarji
	Sunamganj	370	Bilashi Bibi
		371	Bolchan Bibi
		372	Elasi Bibi
		373	Jomila Khatun
		374	Kulsum Bibi
		375	Kushum Debi
		376	Lal Banu
		377	Mon Begum
		378	Mukta Bhanu

		379	Muktaban Bibi
		380	Promila Das
		381	Pyara Begum
		382	Zahera Begum (Hazera)
	Sylhet	383	Chhayarun
		384	Eshnu
		385	Jyotsna

www.ingramcontent.com/pod-product-compliance
Lightning Source LLC
Chambersburg PA
CBHW020522290526
45786CB00002B/727